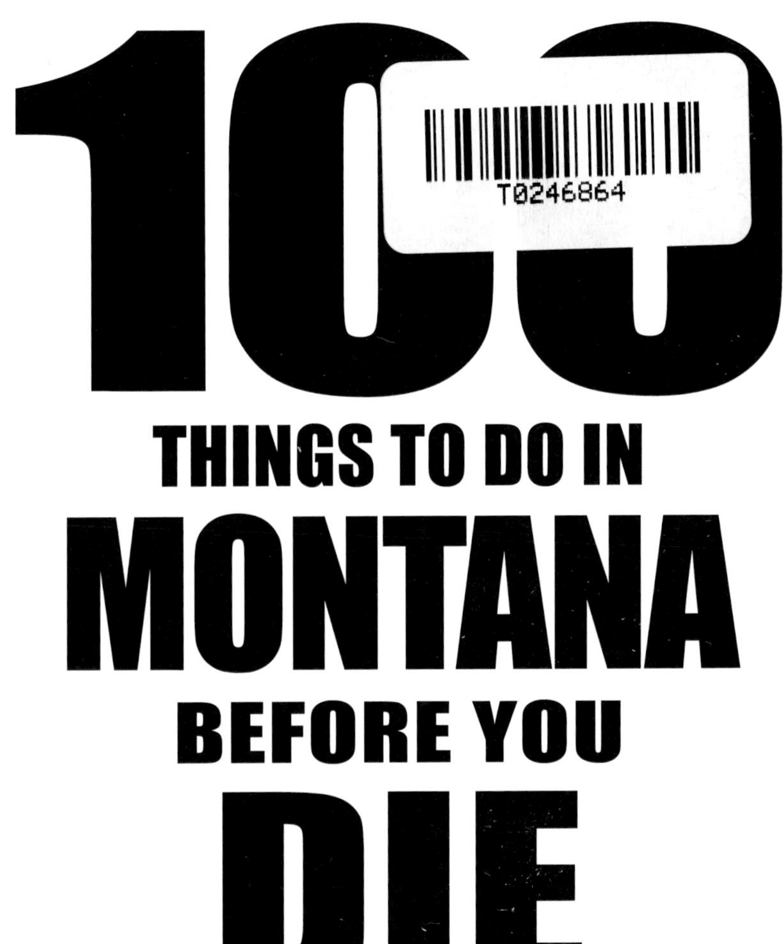

T0246864

100 THINGS TO DO IN MONTANA BEFORE YOU DIE

Sculpture in the Wild

100 THINGS TO DO IN MONTANA BEFORE YOU DIE

SUSIE WALL

Copyright © 2024 by Reedy Press, LLC
Reedy Press
PO Box 5131
St. Louis, MO 63139, USA
www.reedypress.com

No part of this publication may be reproduced or transmitted in any form or by any means, electronic or mechanical, including photocopy, recording, or any information storage and retrieval system, without permission in writing from the publisher.

Permissions may be sought directly from Reedy Press at the above mailing address or via our website at www.reedypress.com.

Library of Congress Control Number: 2023951759

ISBN: 9781681065151

Design by Jill Halpin

All images are by the author unless otherwise noted.

Printed in the United States of America
24 25 26 27 28   5 4 3 2

We (the publisher and the author) have done our best to provide the most accurate information available when this book was completed. However, we make no warranty, guarantee, or promise about the accuracy, completeness, or currency of the information provided, and we expressly disclaim all warranties, express or implied. Please note that attractions, company names, addresses, websites, and phone numbers are subject to change or closure, and this is outside of our control. We are not responsible for any loss, damage, injury, or inconvenience that may occur due to the use of this book. When exploring new destinations, please do your homework before you go. You are responsible for your own safety and health when using this book.

DEDICATION

To Dave, my husband and favorite travel companion. There is no one else I would rather have beside me on the open road.

Bison Range

CONTENTS

Introduction .... **xiii**

Acknowledgments .... **xv**

Food and Drink

1. Dine Aboard the Charlie Russell Chew Choo **2**

2. Feast on a Mountain at the Montana Dinner Yurt **3**

3. Belly Up to Bavaria at Bayern Brewery **4**

4. Pig Out at the Trout Creek Huckleberry Festival **6**

5. Sample Flathead Lake Cheese **7**

6. Satisfy Your Sweet Tooth at Candy Town USA **8**

7. Sit a Spell at Greycliff Mill **10**

8. Sip Flavors of the World at Lake Missoula Tea Company **11**

9. Drink In the Fruits of Tongue River Winery **12**

10. Lunch at Benny's Bistro **14**

11. Chow Down along the Southeast Montana Burger Trail **16**

12. Savor the Tradition of Butte Pasties **17**

13. Wake Up at Montana Coffee Traders **18**

14. Relish the Cherries of Flathead Lake **19**

15. Grab the Napkins at Roadhouse Diner **20**

56. Cruise to Wild Horse Island **100**
57. Raft through the Alberton Gorge **101**
58. Swing across the Kootenai River **102**
59. Ramble among the Giants of Ross Creek **104**
60. Summer on the Slopes in Whitefish **106**
61. Shine a Light on Lewis and Clark Caverns **107**
62. Follow the River's Edge Trail **108**
63. Voyage through Gates of the Mountains **109**
64. Drive the Seeley–Swan **110**

Culture and History

65. Go Below Havre Beneath the Streets **114**
66. Rest Up at Sacajawea Hotel **115**
67. Learn the History behind the Battle of Little Bighorn **116**
68. Walk in the Footsteps of Lewis and Clark **118**
69. Admire the Art of the Forest at Sculpture in the Wild **120**
70. Draw into Pictograph Cave State Park **121**
71. Round 'Em Up at Grant-Kohrs Ranch **122**
72. Take a Tour of Old Butte **124**
73. Dig In at Montana Dinosaur Center **126**
74. View the Art of Charlie Russell **127**

75. Experience Native Culture at Kyiyo Pow Wow....................................**128**
76. Visit Museum of the Rockies....................................**130**
77. Stake Your Claim at Virginia City....................................**131**
78. Serve Time at Old Montana Prison....................................**132**
79. Find Solace at Garden of One Thousand Buddhas....................................**134**
80. Tour the Daly Mansion....................................**135**
81. Travel Back in Time at Bannack State Park....................................**136**
82. Traverse the Great Falls with the Corps of Discovery....................................**138**
83. Stroll through History at Fort Benton....................................**139**
84. Give a Salute to Fort Missoula....................................**140**
85. Discover the Bair Family Museum....................................**142**
86. Stand at the Edge of First Peoples Buffalo Jump....................................**143**

Shopping and Fashion

87. Stir Up Your Inner Chef at Zest....................................**146**
88. Shop 'til You Drop at Rockin Rudy's....................................**147**
89. Peruse the Polebridge Mercantile....................................**148**
90. Read All about It at Country Bookshelf....................................**149**
91. Decorate Your Nest at Birds & Beasleys....................................**150**
92. Tip Your Hat to Western Outdoor....................................**152**
93. Find Bargains at Patagonia Outlet....................................**153**

94. Unearth Treasures in Kehoe's Agate Shop **154**
95. Pamper Yourself at Sage & Cedar **155**
96. Buy Local at Great Gray Gifts **156**
97. Support the Artists of HandMADE Montana **158**
98. Treat Your Feet at Hide & Sole **159**
99. Spark Creativity at Paper and Grace **160**
100. Spend Time in Downtown Livingston **161**

Activities by Season **163**
Suggested Itineraries **167**
Index **171**

INTRODUCTION

I didn't think it was possible for me to love Montana more when I started writing this book. I proved that theory wrong every single trip I took this past year.

I have been traveling and writing about Montana since I moved to Missoula many years ago, so I also thought I knew just about everything there is to know about my home state. Wrong again. Over the 5,962 miles that I drove, and many that I walked, while researching this book, I have learned more about and fell more in love with my home state than I ever thought possible.

I hope that love comes through in my writing. Whether you've lived in Montana your whole life or are visiting for the first time, I also hope this book inspires you to visit as many of the 100 things as possible while on your own travels. And I hope you enjoy them just as much as I did.

Finally, if your favorite "thing" didn't make the book, I truly am sorry. I did the best I could with the time, resources, and knowledge that I had. Instead of ticking things off my own life list, I now have a long list of places I can't wait to return to, and places I didn't get a chance to explore. I would love to chat about your favorite things to do so we can both continue to discover Montana.

— Susie

Greycliff Mill

ACKNOWLEDGMENTS

I would like to thank my husband, Dave Wall, for his endless support and encouragement in all things. I am so lucky that we share a love of travel and exploration. Dave, I can guarantee that I'm planning our next adventure at this very minute.

I would also like to thank my sister, Kathy Piersall, for being my biggest cheerleader in life. She and my brother-in-law, Mark, are two of my favorite people.

Thank you to all my friends in Missoula. Whether I spend every Thanksgiving with you, watch scary movies on my birthday, go birding, hike the trails, discuss books, or play trivia, when I'm not traveling, you make my life rich.

My greatest joy in writing this book, besides having to take road trips for "work," was meeting people from every corner of the state and seeing their passion for Montana on full display. From small-business owners; to people eager to share their talents, cultures, and foods; to folks who simply gave that Montana wave as you passed me on the open road, I thank you. I have lived and traveled many places over the years and I can say without hesitation that Montanans are the friendliest people, and the most incapable of pretense, that you will ever meet.

Big Mountain Ciderworks

FOOD AND DRINK

DINE ABOARD
THE CHARLIE RUSSELL CHEW CHOO

There are few experiences quite like savoring a fine meal in the comfort of a historic train car as you roll across the Montana prairie and the setting sun illuminates the sky.

Revel in this experience aboard the Charlie Russell Chew Choo on a 56-mile round-trip journey along a historic spur track built in 1912. Catch the train 10 miles northwest of Lewistown. During the 4.5-hour journey, feast on a full-course prime rib dinner, including a salad, roasted potatoes, and delectable desserts, while listening to live music and enjoying conversations with your fellow passengers.

Watch out the window for white-tailed deer and pronghorn antelope bounding through the high grass. Hide your valuables as masked train robbers hop the train and regale the crowd with a Wild West gunfight. A vegetarian dinner option is available and alcoholic beverages are provided for an extra charge.

408 E Main St., Lewistown, 406-535-5436
montanadinnertrain.com

TIP

Be sure to book your trip early. Tickets go on sale the first Monday in March for the upcoming season and sell out fast.

2

FEAST ON A MOUNTAIN
AT THE MONTANA DINNER YURT

Tucked away in a pine forest in the mountains above Big Sky Resort, the Montana Dinner Yurt combines great food and a fun adventure.

Your evening begins with a ride up to the yurt, a large circular tent, along a twisting road aboard a retired open-air army truck in the summer or a snowcat in the winter. Once there, relax before dinner on the patio in one of the comfy chairs listening to live music and surrounded by a roaring fire.

Just as your stomach starts to growl, the dinner bell rings, signifying a feast of tender steak cooked to perfection, slathered in peppercorn gravy, savory mashed potatoes, and roasted vegetables. Dessert is a pot of creamy chocolate fondue accompanied by pound cake and fruit for dipping.

Nonalcoholic drinks are included, and you are free to bring your own alcoholic beverage.

PO Box 160496, Big Sky, 406-995-3880
bigskyyurt.com/montana-dinner-yurt

3

BELLY UP TO BAVARIA
AT BAYERN BREWERY

Montana is well known for its craft breweries, and new ones are popping up all the time, but Bayern Brewing in Missoula holds the distinction of being the oldest operating brewery in the state.

Since 1987, Bayern has been brewing beers that celebrate the rich Bavarian heritage of owner and Masterbrewer Jürgen Knöller. Beers are brewed in accordance with the German Law of Purity, meaning only simple ingredients of malted barley, yeast, hops, and water are used.

As the cold fingers of winter set in, savor a pint of their rich Doppelbock Lager. Take in the summer sun on the deck with a refreshing Dump Truck Summer Bock. Feel like a soft and salty pretzel or some authentic German spätzle with your beer? Traditional German dishes using recipes from Jürgen's mother and grandmother are served up on the top floor of the brewery at Edelweiss Bistro.

1507 Montana St., Missoula, 406-721-1482
bayernbrewery.com

OTHER MONTANA BREWERIES

Montana has close to 100 craft breweries spread across the state, and there's not a bad one in the bunch. Here are some of my favorites.

Cross Country Brewing
320 E Allard St.
Glendive, 406-377-BREW
crosscountrybrewing.com

MAP Brewing Company
510 Manley Rd.
Bozeman, 406-587-4070
mapbrewing.com

Cabinet Mountain Brewing Co.
206 Mineral Ave.
Libby, 406-293-BREW
cabinetmountainbrewing.com

Ruby Valley Brew
111 S Main St.
Sheridan, 406-842-5977
rubyvalleybrew.com

Blackfoot River Brewing Company
66 S Park Ave.
Helena, 406-449-3005
blackfootriverbrewing.com

Wildwood Brewing
4018 US Hwy. 93 N
Stevensville, 406-777-2855
wildwoodbrewing.com

2 Basset Brewery
202 E Main St., White Sulphur Springs, 406-547-BEER
2bassetbrewery.com

Philipsburg Brewing Co.
101 W Broadway St.
Philipsburg, 406-859-BREW
philipsburgbrew.com

Smelter City Brewing
101 Main St.
Anaconda, 406-563-0344
facebook.com/smeltercitybrewing

Busted Knuckle Brewery
303 1st Ave. S
Glasgow, 406-228-2277
bustedknucklebrew.com

4

PIG OUT
AT THE TROUT CREEK HUCKLEBERRY FESTIVAL

Wander the forests of western Montana in the late summer and there's a good chance you'll encounter small purple berries nestled within the underbrush.

Congratulations, you've found a huckleberry bush! Slightly smaller than a blueberry with a sweet yet tart flavor, huckleberries only grow wild, and because no one has found a way to cultivate them, huckleberries are a prized commodity when they ripen.

If the thought of huckleberry foraging is too daunting, join the folks in Trout Creek as they celebrate Montana's favorite berry at the annual Huckleberry Festival held the second weekend in August. Gorge on huckleberry ice cream, lemonade, pie, pancakes, and milkshakes. The festival is so much more than food. There's a fun run, a parade, a pie-eating contest, and a kids talent show. Throughout the weekend, listen to live music and browse the booths for huckleberry-inspired jewelry and artwork.

PO Box 1447, Trout Creek, 406-827-7117
huckleberryfestival.com

TIP

You can also purchase bags of just huckleberries at the festival, but it will cost you. In 2023, the going rate for a gallon was $70.

SAMPLE
FLATHEAD LAKE CHEESE

Wendi and Joe Arnold lovingly craft batches of their handmade cow's-milk cheeses just a few blocks from the shores of Flathead Lake in Polson.

Walk up to their convenient tasting window located on the side of their cheese-colored creamery for a visit. Chat with the Arnolds and hear about how they first got the inspiration to make cheese while sitting in their hot tub, and how they use solar panels on the roof to power their operation.

Then it's on to tasting!

Choose from more than 10 varieties of cheese from creamy soft curds to robust firm goudas. Ray's Pop Curds come in flavors like jalapeño and garlic. Joe's Hawaiian Shirt Feta is a salty, tangy addition to any recipe. Revel in all things local with Big Chai Gouda, a collaborative cheese made using Tipu's Chai crafted just down the street.

208 1st Ave. E, Polson, 406-883-0343
flatheadlakecheese.com

6

SATISFY YOUR SWEET TOOTH AT CANDY TOWN USA

No matter if you're a kid or a kid at heart, this massive candy store and soda fountain in Billings has a sweet treat that's just right for you.

The first things you notice when entering Candy Town USA are the colorful towers of licorice, bubble gum, jawbreakers, and spice drops that stretch to the ceiling.

The second thing you notice is the inviting aroma coming from the open kitchen at the back where talented confectioners create all of Candy Town's fudge, nut clusters, and gourmet caramel-dipped apples. What should you choose? The five-pound gummy bear? A basket filled with lollipops and saltwater taffy? Or maybe a bag stuffed with every imaginable flavor of Jelly Belly?

No matter your selection, be sure to save room for a vanilla malt or hot fudge sundae made with love and local Wilcoxson's Ice Cream in the lime sherbet–colored soda fountain.

1025 Shiloh Crossing Blvd., Billings, 406-651-9196
candytownusa.com

OTHER MONTANA CANDY SHOPS

The Sweet Palace
109 E Broadway, Philipsburg, 406-859-3353
sweetpalace.com

Candy Masterpiece Confectionery
120 Central Ave., Great Falls, 406-727-5955
candymasterpiece.com

The Parrot Confectionery
42 N Last Chance Gulch, Helena, 406-442-1470
parrotchocolate.com

The Sweets Barn
11380 US Hwy. 93, Lolo, 406-926-1269
thesweetsbarn.net

Big Sky Candy
319 W Main St., Hamilton, 406-363-0580
bigskycandy.com

Montana Candy Emporium
7 Broadway Ave. N, Red Lodge, 406-446-1119
montanacandyemporium.net

The Old West Antiques & Candy Store
202 S Main St., Darby, 406-821-4076
oldwestcandy.com

SIT A SPELL
AT GREYCLIFF MILL

The Greycliff Mill opened in 2021 just east of Big Timber off I-90 and has since expanded into an interstate oasis you won't want to leave.

Inside the historic barn, watch a gristmill slowly grind locally grown wheat into flour that in turn goes into the delectable pastries you're about to try. Sit on the sun-drenched porch and enjoy a menu of sandwiches, salads, and coffee at the base of the namesake gray cliffs.

Watch ice cream churn and tour the chilly cheese cave at the creamery just past the barn. Kids will enjoy making wooden toys in the craft shop. The whole family can fish in the spring-fed trout pond and ride horses to the top of the cliffs.

Finding it hard to hit the road? Book one of seven Airbnbs on the property so you can wake up and do it all over again.

11 Greycliff Creek Ln., Greycliff, 406-930-0870
greycliffmill.com

SIP FLAVORS OF THE WORLD
AT LAKE MISSOULA TEA COMPANY

Whether the middle of winter or the height of summer, stop into Lake Missoula Tea Company in downtown Missoula to savor a variety of teas grown around the globe.

Owners Heather and Jake Kreilick travel to farms from Colombia to Taiwan sourcing the finest teas, which they then bring home to create their unique loose-leaf blends.

Grab a seat at the "tea bar" and order a cup of any of their hot or chilled teas. Try a tea-based drink such as House Chai or London Fog, Earl Grey blended with cream and honey. Then choose from 150 different teas and blends to brew at home.

Varieties include black, green, rooibos, oolong, and seasonal blends. Need a vessel from which to drink all this fabulous tea? Lake Missoula also sells a wide range of accessories from kettles to travel tea sets to strainers.

136 E Broadway, Missoula, 406-926-1038
lakemissoulateacompany.com

9

DRINK IN THE FRUITS
OF TONGUE RIVER WINERY

Look no further than Tongue River Winery as the perfect example of Montana ingenuity. Since 2010, Bob and Marilyn Thaden have been producing award-winning wine from soil to bottle on their picturesque piece of land in Miles City along the unforgiving eastern plains.

A true labor of love, they plant, harvest, press, and bottle close to 1,000 cases of wine each year. When you're in the area, a visit to Tongue River for a tasting and a chat with the affable couple is a must. All their wine comes solely from Montana fruit and grapes, most of which are grown on-site and able to withstand winter temperatures that can plummet to 40 below zero.

Enjoy a taste of the dry Oaky Choke made from barrel-aged chokecherries, their semisweet Ripe Apple, and the Frontenac Gris consisting of winter-hearty hybrid grapes, then stock up on several bottles to indulge once you're home.

99 Morning Star Ln., Miles City, 406-853-1028
tongueriverwinery.com

TIP

The winery hours are "Any reasonable time" and "Any day except Sunday morning." Send Bob an email at bob@tongueriverwinery.com if you know when you'll be there, or you can call the cell numbers posted on the door when you drop by.

OTHER MONTANA WINERIES

Ten Spoon Vineyard and Winery
4175 Rattlesnake Dr.
Missoula, 406-549-8703
tenspoon.com

Hidden Legend Winery
1345 US Hwy. 93 N, #5
Victor, 406-363-6323
hiddenlegendwinery.com

Shed Horn Cellars
335 W Main St.
Hamilton, 406-361-9532
shedhorncellars.com

Blodgett Canyon Cellars
111 W Main St.
Hamilton, 406-531-7444
blodgettcanyoncellar.com

White Raven Winery
7457 US Hwy. 2 E
Columbia Falls, 406-797-7229
whiteravenwinery.com

Unleashed: A Winery
20 Spokane Ave.
Whitefish, 406-730-8558
unleashedwinery.com

Waters Edge Winery & Bistro
2593 US Hwy. 2 E, #8
Kalispell, 406-314-4193
wewinerykalispell.com

MontaVino Winery & Tasting Room
38 1st Ave. E, Ste. D
Kalispell, 406-300-1330
montavinowinery.com

Blend
31 S Willson
Bozeman, 406-414-9693
blendbzn.com

Valhalla Meadery
875 Bridger Dr., Unit B
Bozeman, 406-577-2383
valhallabozeman.com

Yellowstone Cellars & Winery
1335 Holiday Cir.,
Billings, 406-281-8400
yellowstonecellars.com

10

LUNCH
AT BENNY'S BISTRO

Much is said about breakfast being the most important meal of the day, but at Benny's Bistro in downtown Helena, the midday meal shines.

Plate-sized salads piled high with fresh ingredients and luscious satisfying soups give you all the energy you need without weighing you down for an afternoon exploring Montana's capital city.

As a bonus, supporting local farmers and following sustainable practices are of utmost importance to the folks at Benny's. Dip a slice of soft fresh-baked bread into a bowl of tomato soup kissed with hints of rosemary and just the right amount of cream.

Ready your fork for the house salad covered in candied pecans, pumpkin seeds, and apple slices, all drizzled with a tart balsamic vinaigrette. The lunch menu also features piping-hot paninis and bowls of red and green curry, and each diner is rewarded with a sweet, buttery madeleine cookie on the side.

108 E 6th Ave., Helena, 406-443-0105
bennyshelena.com

Benny's Bistro

11

CHOW DOWN
ALONG THE SOUTHEAST MONTANA BURGER TRAIL

Take a bite out of Montana's thriving beef industry along the Southeast Montana Burger Trail that stretches from Billings to Wibaux, just 10 miles from the North Dakota border.

Celebrating small towns like Ekalaka, Forsyth, and Acton, the trail currently consists of 24 stops where the staff have concocted the perfect burger to make the locals come running.

Sample the trail at your leisure or make a goal to hit every stop. You'll need a knife and fork, and possibly a spoon, at the Homestead Inn in Broadview to best savor the open-faced Mexi Burger slathered in the owner's secret green chili recipe.

Just try to get your hands around the Roy Rogers Bar Grill & Casino's burger piled high with a fried green tomato and thick bacon in the historic town of Terry, population 550.

southeastmontana.com/burgertrail

SAVOR THE TRADITION
OF BUTTE PASTIES

For years, men from many different countries sought work in the silver and copper mines of Butte, often bringing with them their families, traditions, and foods.

Few of these culinary traditions are more reflective of this time than the Irish pasty. This savory meat pie was made by scores of Irish wives and mothers as a filling and packable meal for their men as they headed out to a long shift below ground.

Today, you can enjoy pasties above ground, minus the backbreaking work, at many establishments in Butte. Traditional pasties consist of tender chunks of beef tossed with diced potatoes and wrapped up in a flaky half-moon-shaped pastry, and often served alongside rich brown gravy for topping.

Many places put their own unique spin on the traditional recipe, so it's a good idea to try them all.

Joe's Pasty Shop
1641 Grand Ave., Butte
406-723-9071
facebook.com/joespasty

The Pasty Place
2810 Pine St., Butte
406-565-9169
facebook.com/profile.php?id=100088936072474

Town Talk Bakery
611 E Front St., Butte
406-782-4985
facebook.com/ttbinc59701

Truzzolino Tamales
1921 Harrison Ave., Butte
406-782-0374
facebook.com/truzzolinotamales

WAKE UP
AT MONTANA COFFEE TRADERS

Montana Coffee Traders helps people power up for a day of adventures at their flagship roastery and café in Whitefish.

Inside this unassuming farmhouse along Highway 93, arabica coffees from around the world are roasted to perfection resulting in steaming cups of caffeine served up in delectable ways, from the robust earthy Grizzly Blend to the sweet vanilla Glacier Blend.

Other varieties include Huckleberry, Organic Sumatra Dark, and the smoky Organic Dusk 'Til Dawn. While waiting for your drink order, shop for brewing accessories like filters, coffee grinders, mugs, locally made art, and bags of coffee to take home.

Proud to be a part of their communities, Montana Coffee Traders focuses on sustainability, being a good employer in the region, and maintaining a respectful relationship with the international growers they work with.

5810 US Hwy. 93 S, Whitefish, 406-862-7628
110 Central Ave., Whitefish, 406-862-7667
30 9th St. W, Columbia Falls, 406-892-7696
111 S Main St., Kalispell, 406-756-2326
coffeetraders.com

14

RELISH THE CHERRIES
OF FLATHEAD LAKE

As the dry, hot days of July roll around, fruit-loving folks of western Montana begin to dream about biting into fat, juicy, and oh-so-sweet Flathead Lake cherries.

Dozens of independently owned cherry orchards dot the shores surrounding Flathead Lake, with the highest concentration on the eastern side between Bigfork and Polson.

When cherries are plentiful in late July through early September, you'll find many growers setting up stands along the highways selling Lapin, Rainier, and Lambert cherries.

If you only have time for one stop, pull into Bowman Orchards, 10 miles south of Bigfork. The Bowman family has been growing cherries here for over a century, finding unique ways to share their bounty.

Pick up canned cherries cradled in a light syrup, perfect for baking a pie, or grab a bottle of their cherry wine, perfect for pairing with your bowl of blushing cherries.

19944 Montana Hwy. 35, Bigfork, 406-982-3246
bowmancherryorchards.com

15

GRAB THE NAPKINS
AT ROADHOUSE DINER

Welcome to the Roadhouse Diner, where the awards and accolades heaped upon owners Tara and Jason Beam's famous burgers almost outnumber the tables inside this beloved Great Falls restaurant.

The two-page menu features just 10 burgers crafted to perfection, along with a special burger of the day, a chance to build your own burger, and a few pork, chicken, and vegetarian options.

A big key to Roadhouse's success is the Beams commitment to using local ingredients, including beef sourced from the McCafferty Ranch in nearby Belt, just 30 miles away.

Try the classic Roadhouse Burger topped with American cheese, pickles, and grilled onions, or go wild with the quirky PB&J Burger. Each burger is served wrapped in paper to catch all the yummy juices and dripping house-made sauces, and paired with shoestring fries you can't seem to stop popping in your mouth.

613 15th St. N, Great Falls, 406-788-8839
roadhousegf.com

16

TASTE ITALY
AT FRONT STREET MARKET

Since 1990, the Front Street Market in Butte has been offering the flavors of Italy through a variety of unique ingredients and specialty wines.

Stroll the wondrous aisles of this locally owned grocery store to shop for a diverse selection of dry and fresh pastas, savory rich sauces, exotic vinegars, flavored olive oils, salty cured meats, fiery spices, and nutty cheeses, many of which are imported from Italy and found nowhere else in Montana.

Whether you consider yourself a seasoned cook or just starting out in the kitchen, owners Jim and Marla Yakawich are always ready to help you find the right ingredients so you can whip up your own Italian feast.

Don't feel like cooking? Grab a seat in their deli and order up a juicy sandwich, or select a refrigerated tray of fresh lasagna or ravioli made on-site to take home to the family.

8 W Front St., Butte, 406-782-2614
facebook.com/frontstreetmarket

17

ENJOY THE BOUNTY
OF BIG MOUNTAIN CIDERWORKS

Imagine savoring a crisp glass of cider while looking outside at the very fruit trees responsible for this delectable concoction.

Become a part of this scene at the family-owned-and-operated Big Mountain Ciderworks located among the farm fields of northwest Kalispell. A staggering variety of apples and pears are grown in Big Mountain's orchard, then used to make distinctive hard cider in the gleaming tanks of their cidery.

Visit the lively taproom for a taste of Newtown Pippin, a dry apple cider with a champagne hint, or MoonGlow Pear, made using pears and apples with just the right amount of sweet.

Pair your cider with a basket of french fries or huckleberry and goat cheese flatbread from the food menu. For the perfect experience, take a seat on the patio on a warm summer evening and watch the sun set over the mountains.

1051 Old Reserve Dr., Kalispell, 406-260-4212
bigmountaincider.com

OTHER MONTANA CIDERIES

Western Cider Co.
501 N California St., Missoula, 406-540-4477
westerncider.com

Last Chance Pub & Cider Mill
2203 Montana Ave., Billings, 406-534-8918
lastchancecider.com

Lockhorn Cider House
21 S Wallace Ave., Bozeman, 406-580-9098
lockhornhardcider.com

Rough Cut Hard Cider
3250 US Hwy. 2 E, Kalispell, 406-257-8886
roughcuthardcider.com

Backroad Cider
facebook.com/backroadcider406

EAT DESSERT FIRST
AT IRON HORSE CAFE & PIE SHOP

Delectable pies are the star of the menu at this lively diner on the corner of Main and Birch Streets in Three Forks.

All the standards are here like cherry, coconut, and strawberry rhubarb, but you'll also find some wonderfully creative pie creations like raspberry lemonade, s'more, and monster cookie.

Pies are made daily by owner Jamie Taylor, lovingly known as the Three Forks Pie Lady, using only fresh ingredients and highlighting what's in season. Sink your fork into the Lemon Lime Margarita pie, a luscious tart cream pie on a graham cracker crust. Savor a slice of the Bourbon Pecan, a house favorite combining crunchy nuts and a rich gooey filling.

More than just pie, the Iron Horse carries their pledge of using fresh ingredients to the breakfast, lunch, and dinner menus with diner standards like cheesy omelets, creamy soups, and juicy burgers.

24 Main St., Three Forks, 406-285-4455
ironhorsecafetf.com

TIP
Iron Horse also offers gluten-free pie options. Check out their Facebook page for daily pie and food specials.
facebook.com/ironhorsecafeandpieshop

19

COME HOME
TO MISSION BISTRO

After years spent working in big-city, upscale restaurants, siblings Angie and Eric Loessberg returned to their hometown of Stevensville, opening Mission Bistro to share their passion for good food with their former neighbors. The menu features elements of French and Northwest cuisines. Many items rotate with the seasons, but you'll always find steak, chicken, pasta, and vegetarian options featuring local ingredients.

Start your meal with a salad topped with Amaltheia goat cheese from Belgrade, or a comforting bowl of their signature French onion soup, and a basket of warm Le Petit bread from Missoula. Grab your steak knife and dig into the bacon-wrapped filet nestled beside pillowy mashed potatoes.

Save room for dessert like huckleberry cheesecake or triple chocolate torte with a berry glaze. Since opening, the bistro has built quite a following of devoted local customers, so reservations are a must.

225 Main St., Stevensville, 406-777-6945
missionbistromt.com

TIP

The bistro is also famous for its Sunday brunch. Choose from savory eggs Benedict with Redneck ham from Kalispell or sweet French toast with orange zest and huckleberry syrup.

20

FORAGE
AT MISSOULA'S FARMERS MARKETS

You'll find farmers markets celebrating local farmers and food producers in most towns across Montana. Missoula takes it to the next level, boasting four separate markets in the summer.

Higgins Avenue is the place to be on Saturdays from May to early October as the founding Missoula Farmers' Market operates on the north end of the avenue, while the Clark Fork River Market sets up a few blocks south.

Walk from one to the other, or catch the free trolley that travels between the two. On Sundays, you'll find the Target Range Farmers Market, and on Thursdays, the Orchard Homes Farmers Market is underway.

The selections at each market include locally grown produce like apples, lettuce, and tomatoes, as well as eggs, cuts of meat, and fresh-baked goods. Be sure to strike up conversations with the friendly vendors eager to chat about their wares.

Missoula Farmers' Market
North end of Higgins Ave., Missoula
703-772-2792
missoulafarmersmarket.org

Clark Fork River Market
101 Carousel Dr., Missoula
406-880-9648
clarkforkmarket.com

Target Range Farmers Market
4095 S Ave. W, Missoula
406-728-5302
facebook.com/
targetrangefarmersmarket

Orchard Homes Farmers Market
2537 S 3rd St. W, Missoula
406-370-0375
facebook.com/
orchardhomesfarmersmarket

21

SHAKE IT UP
AT WESTSLOPE DISTILLERY

Westslope Distillery in Hamilton creates one-of-a-kind spirits, while keeping with their strong commitment to community by partnering with local growers and producers to source many of their ingredients.

Sweet Sting Honey Spirit uses mead from Hidden Legend Winery in nearby Victor, which in turn uses Montana honey to make their mead, all resulting in a crisp and light brandy concoction.

"Brum" is Westslope's version of a light Caribbean rum combining Montana sugar beets and honey. Spirit varieties also include whiskey, gin, and vodka. Savor one of their many unique cocktails from a comfy chair in their warm and welcoming tasting room.

The menu is ever evolving to celebrate the flavors of the season, and standard options are always available for the classic cocktail connoisseur. Before you depart, be sure to stock up on a few bottles to enjoy at home.

172 S 2nd St., Hamilton, 406-375-5590
westslopedist.com

MONTANA DISTILLERIES

Much like breweries, Montana has too many distilleries to mention. Here are some of my favorites.

Whistling Andy Distillery
8020 Montana Hwy. 35
Bigfork, 406-837-2620
whistlingandy.com

Glacier Distilling Company
10237 US Hwy. 2 E
Coram, 406-387-9887
glacierdistilling.com

Willie's Distillery
312 E Main St.
Ennis, 406-682-4117
williesdistillery.com

Spotted Bear Spirits
503 Railway St.
Whitefish, 406-730-2436
spottedbearspirits.com

Montgomery Distillery
129 W Front St.
Missoula, 406-926-1725
montgomerydistillery.com

Stonehouse Distillery
37 Muffley Ln.
Winston, 406-465-2816
stonehouse-distillery.com

Wildrye Distilling
111 E Oak St., Ste. 1E
Bozeman, 406-577-2288
wildryedistilling.com

Headframe Spirits
21 S Montana St.
Butte, 406-299-2886
headframespirits.com

Lolo Creek Distillery
6610 US Hwy 12 W
Lolo, 406-926-2803
lolocreekdistillery.com

22

SLICE
INTO EUGENE'S PIZZA

Eugene's Pizza has been serving up its delicious creations to the Glasgow community since 1962. You're sure to find it packed with devoted locals seven days a week.

Eugene E. Barger opened the pizzeria in 1962. Five years later, Arlie and Mary Sue Knodel purchased Eugene's, retaining the name and the tradition of serving up tasty pies topped with fresh ingredients. Eugene's remains in its original location, and in the Knodel family, to this day after sons Jeff and Sam took the reins in 1992.

The pizza's signature crust is crisp, flaky, and sturdy enough to support a mound of toppings. Tip your hat to Glasgow's ranching community with Jeff's Special, a meat-and-potato pizza topped with ground beef and tater tots. Sam's Special switches out the tots for juicy pineapple. The Henry "J" goes wild with Canadian bacon and sauerkraut, and the Vegetable Gonzo pizza says it all.

193 Klein Ave., Glasgow, 406-228-8552
eugenespizza.com

Eugene's Pizza

Bitterroot Celtic Games & Gathering

MUSIC
AND ENTERTAINMENT

23

HEAR THE PIPE AND DRUM
AT THE CELTIC FESTIVAL

Welcome, lads and lasses, to the annual Bitterroot Celtic Games & Gathering! This lively festival celebrates Celtic heritage, history, and tradition the third weekend of each August on the grounds of the Daly Mansion in Hamilton.

Cheer on burly men in kilts throwing massive wooden beams at the caber toss. Listen to the haunting sounds of bagpipes from pipe and drum bands from across the state.

Clap along to fiddle players as Irish and Highland dancers kick up their heels. Browse dozens of booths to shop for gleaming swords, pewter beer steins, and woolen clothing. Drink up to Celtic tradition at the tea, scotch, and mead tastings.

Be sure not to miss the opening ceremonies held both Saturday and Sunday at 1 p.m., when proud representatives from clans with names such as Ogilvie, MacKay, and Cian show off their colors.

251 Eastside Hwy., Hamilton, 406-274-8886
bcgg.org

TIP

Purchase tickets to the festival online before you go to avoid the long lines at the gate.

LAUGH UNTIL YOUR SIDES SPLIT

AT BREWERY FOLLIES

Hilarity ensues at the Brewery Follies, Virginia City's live comedy show. Twice a day from Memorial Day weekend through September, this talented troupe of comedians sing, dance, and let the jokes fly inside the historic H. S. Gilbert Brewery building, Montana's first brewery, established in 1863 in Montana's once thriving territorial capital.

Let's get this out of the way at the start: this is not a show for children. There is no nudity, but you're sure to blush and guffaw all at once at the bawdy gags, adult humor, and timely satire. Those easily offended should consider enjoying a family-oriented performance down the street with the Virginia City Players.

The follies have been running since 1984. Many beloved performers return year after year, but the routines never get old. Reservations are made by phone only and tickets sell out fast.

200 E Cover St., Virginia City, 800-829-2969, ext. 3
breweryfollies.net

25

SPIN
ON THE GREAT NORTHERN CAROUSEL

Kids of every age will squeal with delight while whirling around on the Great Northern Carousel, located in Helena's Great Northern Town Center.

Both an amusement ride and a work of art, the carousel features 37 hand-carved, hand-painted creatures native to Montana, plus the traditional, yet still exquisite, horses.

Admire the decorative panels of stained glass atop the carousel that depict several of Helena's beloved landmarks. Saddle up on a bucking cutthroat trout, a roaring grizzly bear, a leaping frog, or a prancing pronghorn as the carousel turns at an exhilarating six rotations per minute.

Open year-round, the carousel is always a bright place to play on a dark winter day. When you're ready for a break, grab an ice cream cone or a slice of pizza in the snack bar while you decide which animal to hop aboard next.

989 Carousel Way, Helena, 406-457-5353
gncarousel.com

OTHER MONTANA CAROUSELS

A Carousel for Missoula
101 Carousel Dr., Missoula, 406-549-8382
carouselformissoula.com

Spirit of Columbia Gardens Carousel
3105 Utah St., Butte, 406-494-7775
facebook.com/profile.php?id=100064548947497

Carousel Rest Area of Shelby
441 11th Ave. N, Shelby, 406-424-8444
shelbycarousel.wixsite.com/shelby

26

CATCH A SHOW
AT KETTLEHOUSE AMPHITHEATER

Listen to amazing live music with a local brew in hand at the Kettlehouse Amphitheater in the tiny town of Bonner, just outside of Missoula.

Kettlehouse Brewing Company had been a favorite among local beer lovers for many years when the owners realized that the land next to their production facility in Bonner along the Blackfoot River had great potential for an outdoor music venue.

Several nights a week from May until September, you can now enjoy a concert put on by a wide range of musical acts from Little Big Town to Béla Fleck to Slayer. Big names sell out fast, but tickets are fairly easy to acquire for many others.

Arrive early to get a pint of Double Haul IPA or Cold Smoke Scotch Ale. Secure your spot on the grassy lawn to people-watch before the show starts and you dance the night away.

605 Cold Smoke Ave., Bonner, 406-830-4640
logjampresents.com/venue/kettlehouse-amphitheater

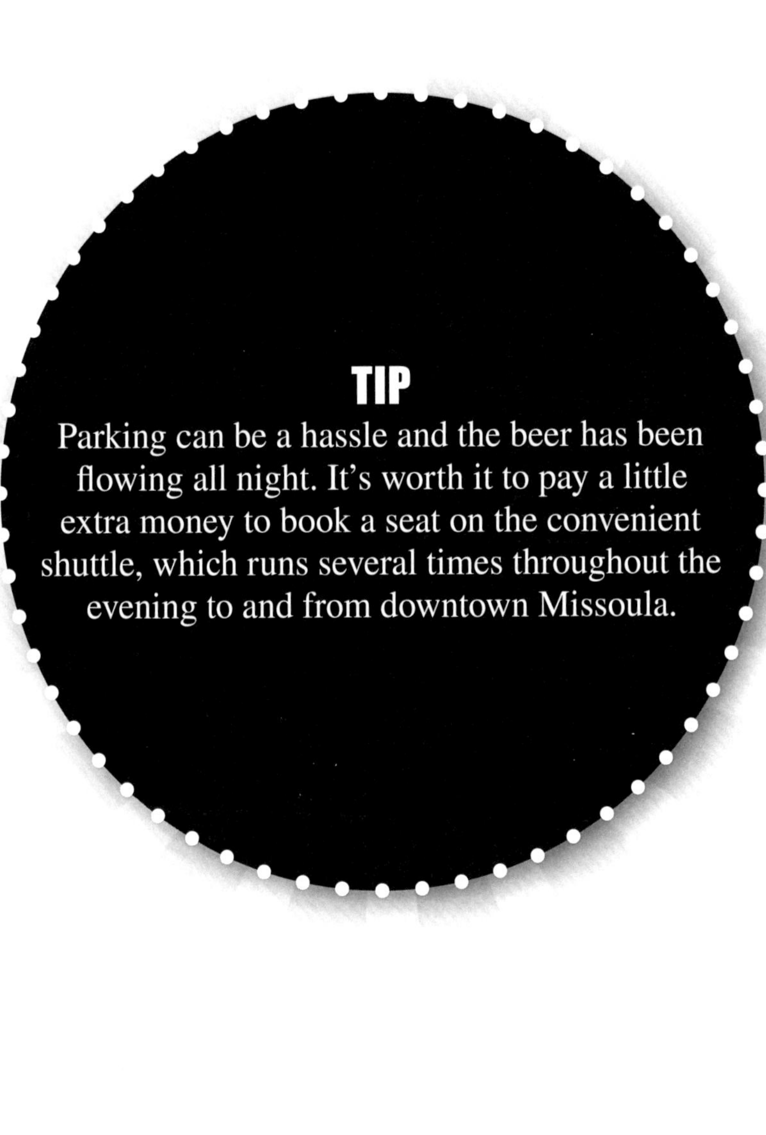

TIP

Parking can be a hassle and the beer has been flowing all night. It's worth it to pay a little extra money to book a seat on the convenient shuttle, which runs several times throughout the evening to and from downtown Missoula.

27

BELIEVE IN MERMAIDS
AT THE SIP 'N DIP LOUNGE

What better way to spend a chilly Montana evening than lounging in a tiki bar being entertained by mermaids frolicking in a pool before your very eyes.

Located in downtown Great Falls inside the O'Haire Inn, the allure of Sip 'n Dip's wide selection of fruity umbrella drinks is reason enough to visit this legendary lounge, but it's the chance to view fish-tailed mermaids swimming in the pool behind the window of the bar that really draws in the crowds.

The mermaids, and occasionally mermen, pose for pictures as they wave and blow kisses to the patrons. Catch these bathing beauties seven days a week beginning at 6 p.m.

Those under 21 years of age are allowed until 8 p.m., but be advised, this is a dark, loud, and sometimes rowdy bar serving drinks like the Drunken Monkey and Swamp Water, sure to guarantee a blissful buzz.

17 7th St. S, Great Falls, 406-454-2141
ohairemotorinn.com/sip-n-dip

LISTEN TO WOLVES
AT HOWLERS INN

Imagine awaking from your slumber to the sound of howling wolves just outside your window. Your dreams become reality at Howlers Inn Bed & Breakfast and Wolf Sanctuary located on a sweeping hillside just outside Bozeman.

Proprietors Thomas and Charlene lovingly care for five captive-bred wolves on their property that are unable to be released into the wild. They do everything in their power to help them remain "wolfy," as Thomas says.

Book a stay at the bed-and-breakfast for close-up views of these majestic creatures while you relax on the wide porch overlooking the sprawling natural sanctuary.

The inn also boasts a large community room full of games and guidebooks to help you discover the wealth of adventures in the area, if only you can tear yourself away from the wolves.

3185 Jackson Creek Rd., Bozeman, 406-587-2050
howlersinn.com

WALK ON THE WILD SIDE
AT ZOOMONTANA

Montana's only zoo is found on 70 sprawling acres in the outskirts of Billings. In addition to being a zoo, it is also a botanical garden, accredited arboretum, and education facility.

Stroll through the lush grounds past native trees and plants to view more than 80 animals including Amur tigers, red pandas, river otters, wolverines, and grizzly bears. Be sure to listen for the haunting howls of the gray wolves.

Most of the animals are rescues, and all of them reside in enclosures that mimic their natural environments as much as possible, including climate.

ZooMontana only places animals that are found along the 45th parallel of Earth in outside enclosures, which makes them more than capable of handling harsh Montana winters. Inside the warm education building, you'll find a wide range of reptiles, birds, and Winston, the two-toed sloth.

2100 S Shiloh Rd., Billings, 406-652-8100
zoomontana.org

TIP

For a special treat, attend one of the many events that ZooMontana puts on throughout the year, from holiday light displays to outdoor concerts to a beer festival. Check their website for upcoming dates.

ZooMontana

30

FERRY
ACROSS THE MISSOURI RIVER

The Upper Missouri River cuts through the heart of central Montana. Crossing its treacherous waters was once a monumental task until the Carter River Ferry was established in 1917 as a safe way to transport automobiles from bank to bank.

Today, you can take a free ride on one of three ferries outside Carter, Virgelle, and Winifred. Ferries generally operate seven days a week from spring to fall as weather allows.

Drive up to the landing and follow the posted instructions to signal the ferry operator, usually with a honk of the horn. When ready, the operator motions you to drive aboard. Take in the magnificent views as the chugging motor slowly pulls you and the ferry along cables that span the wide river.

Be sure to bring an accurate map to navigate the remote rural roads from the highway to the ferry and back once across the river.

Carter Ferry
Ferry Rd., Carter

Virgelle Ferry
8337 Virgelle Ferry Rd. N, Loma

McClelland/Stafford Ferry
Stafford Ferry Rd., Winifred

TIP

The gracious ferry operators are more than happy to give you a ride and offer directions back to the highway, but please remember this is their home and many locals use the ferry as a source of transportation. Be respectful of everyone's time, and be sure to say a big thanks for the great ride. A monetary donation to help with the operation of the ferry is always a kind gesture.

31

BRIGHTEN YOUR DAY
AT TIZER BOTANIC GARDENS

You could spend hours happily getting lost within the six lush acres of Tizer Botanic Gardens & Arboretum just outside Jefferson City.

Smell the staggering variety of flowers, identify the cascading leaves of shade trees, and listen to the calming sounds of Prickly Pear Creek at one of only three internationally accredited arboretums, or botanical gardens, in the state.

The grounds incorporate more than 10 separate gardens, each highlighting its own unique flora. Little ones can look for spirits of the forest hiding among the fanciful blooms in the Children's Garden.

Watch colorful winged creatures flit from flower to flower in the Hummingbird and Butterfly Garden. Breathe in the enticing aromas in the Rose Garden, then take a short climb up the Wildflower Walk to the observation deck where you can take in all the beauty below.

38 Tizer Lake Rd., Jefferson City, 406-933-8789
tizergardens.com

Tizer Botanic Gardens

SING ALONG
AT BIGFORK SUMMER PLAYHOUSE

Come see this talented group of performers sing and dance through toe-tapping musicals at the Bigfork Summer Playhouse.

This repertory theater company puts on five to six lavish productions from June to Labor Day weekend, ending the season with the popular *Hits of the 50s, 60s and 70s* rock-and-roll extravaganza.

The schedule changes each year and guarantees a varied lineup of shows ranging from the powerful *Fiddler on the Roof* to the irreverent *Monty Python's Spamalot*. Several past and present performers hail from the area, and many have gone on to successful careers on the stage and screen like Missoula's Academy Award–winning actor, J. K. Simmons.

Little ones will enjoy watching many of the summer productions. If they're interested in more than just watching, the Bigfork Playhouse Children's Theater gives them an opportunity to come on stage during the school year.

526 Electric Ave., Bigfork, 406-837-4886
bigforksummerplayhouse.com

OTHER MONTANA COMMUNITY THEATERS YOU WON'T WANT TO MISS

Missoula Community Theatre
200 N Adams St., Missoula, 406-728-1911
mctinc.org

Fort Peck Summer Theatre
201 Missouri Ave., Fort Peck, 406-526-9943
fortpecktheatre.org

Cutler Bros. Productions
301 Main St., Deer Lodge, 406-846-4096
cutlerbros.com

The Playmill
29 Madison Ave., West Yellowstone, 406-646-7757
playmill.com

Grandstreet Theatre
325 N Park Ave., Helena, 406-447-1574
grandstreettheatre.com

33

GAZE UP
AT THE TRAIL TO THE STARS

You could go just about anywhere in central and eastern Montana to escape light pollution, but to easily find the best spots, download Montana's Trail to the Stars map.

You won't find palatial mansions of Hollywood stars on this map, just wide-open spaces and sparsely populated towns where stargazers are surrounded by some of the darkest skies in the country.

Set a goal to follow the entire trail or pick from the areas you'll be passing through on your travels. Forty-six sites are currently on the map and span from the Rocky Mountain Front, west of Great Falls, to Brush Lake State Park in the northeast corner of the state. Stops include lakeshores, parks, badlands, and campgrounds.

The website also includes a link to stargazing events and a night sky calculator so you can input information about your trip and maximize your dark sky experience.

trailtothestars.com

TIP

Download and print out a copy of the map before setting out as there is little to no chance of getting Internet service at these remote sites.

CELEBRATE THE SEASON
IN RED LODGE

Come join the fun-loving citizens of Red Lodge as they party in the streets, kicking off the holiday season during the annual Christmas Stroll.

The festivities are held on the first Friday and Saturday evenings of December when Broadway Avenue is blocked off to make way for yuletide joy.

The Community Lantern Walk starts the celebration, followed by the Blade Parade, where brightly lit machines capable of plowing Red Lodge's substantial snowfalls rumble down the street each evening.

Then here comes Santa in a horse-drawn wagon on his way to the Beartooth Elks Lodge where he'll listen to children's Christmas wishes. The merriment continues as bonfires light up the street, carolers serenade the crowds, and horse-drawn wagons pull rosy-cheeked revelers.

Be sure to bring your Christmas list since the shops along Broadway stay open late offering holiday specials and yummy treats.

Broadway Ave., Red Lodge, 406-446-1718
redlodge.com/red-lodge-christmas-stroll.asp

RACE TO WHITEFISH
FOR SKIJORING

Come to Whitefish to catch the exciting spectacle of skijoring, a combination of two favorite Montana outdoor activities: skiing and horseback riding.

It's interesting to note that the word "skijoring" derives from "ski" and the Norwegian word *kjøring*, meaning "to drive." But all you really need to know is that you are about to witness one of the most extreme and thrilling competitions on snow as a horseback rider galloping at top speed pulls a skier through a course littered with jumps and turns.

Each winter, tournaments are held throughout Montana in winter meccas such as Wisdom, Lewistown, and Big Sky, with one of the largest races on the schedule in Whitefish.

Whitefish welcomes spectators to the skijoring event as a kickoff to their festive Whitefish Winter Carnival that features a parade, parties, and the Penguin Plunge, when costumed revelers jump into the icy waters of Whitefish Lake.

whitefishskijoring.org

Whitefish Winter Carnival
PO Box 364, Whitefish
whitefishwintercarnival.com

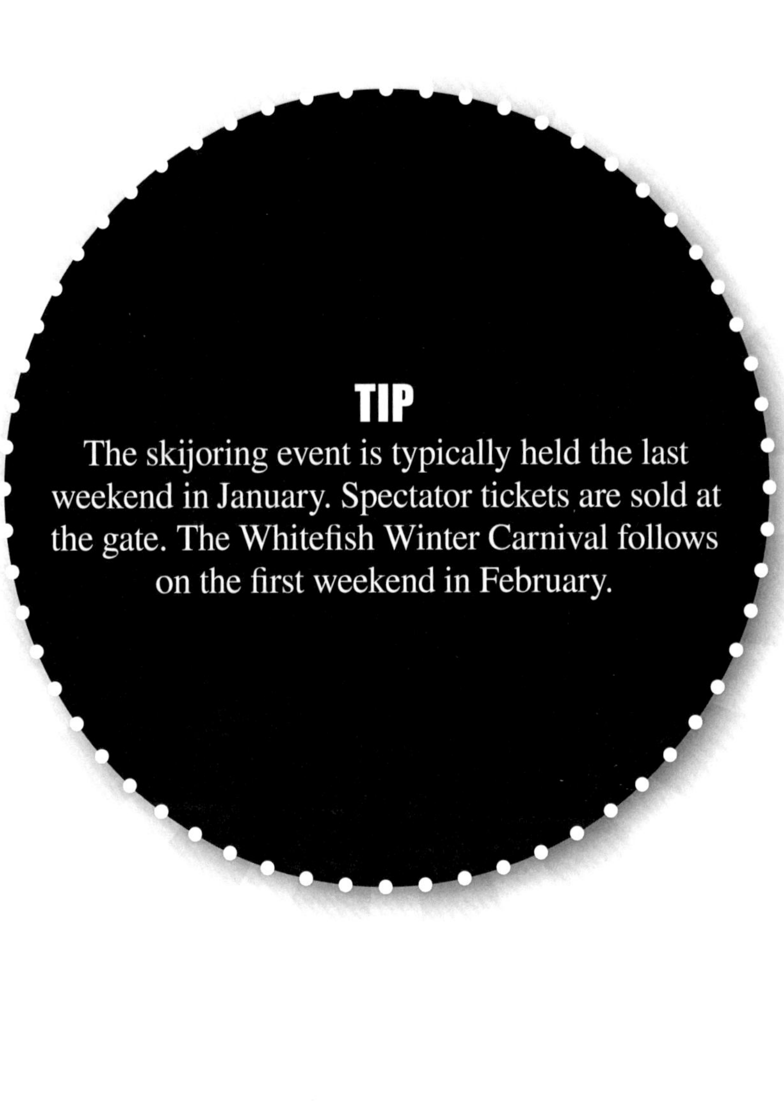
TIP
The skijoring event is typically held the last weekend in January. Spectator tickets are sold at the gate. The Whitefish Winter Carnival follows on the first weekend in February.

GET TECHNICAL
AT AMERICAN COMPUTER & ROBOTICS MUSEUM

Notable scientist Dr. Edward O. Wilson once called this fascinating and quirky museum, "Inch for inch, the best museum in the world."

Tucked away in the corner of a Bozeman office park, the museum is a treasure trove of technology that leads you through 4,000 years of human innovation including 17th-century prints of Shakespeare's *Macbeth* and Ralph Baer's "Brown Box," a prototype for the world's first video game.

A knowledge guide will start you off with a brief tour then set you free to explore. Marvel at an original Apple computer donated by Apple Inc. cofounder Steve Wozniak. The *Man on the Moon* exhibit showcases the Minuteman 1 Missile Flight Computer. Learn the science of codes in the cryptology room where the World War II Enigma Machine is deciphered.

Head over to the robotics exhibit where you'll come face-to-face with *Forbidden Planet*'s Robby the Robot.

2023 Stadium Dr., Ste. 1-A, Bozeman, 406-582-1288
acrmuseum.org

STEP
THROUGH THE MONTANA VORTEX

Visit the Montana Vortex and House of Mystery in Columbia Falls to question all you thought you knew about the physical world in a fun and lighthearted environment.

Check in at the gift shop and sign up for a tour offered several times a day mid-May through September. While waiting to begin, browse the extensive gift shop full of local art, crystals, and Bigfoot and UFO souvenirs.

Your tour guide will then bring you into the lovely forest behind the shop where it is believed three powerful vortexes, or energy fields, exist. Experience these vortexes through a series of fascinating and thought-provoking physical experiments to demonstrate that power.

You'll then enter the wild and wonderful crooked House of Mystery. It's hard to stop giggling as you attempt to walk from end to end, stand on steps, and climb a ladder while your body tilts at dizzying angles.

7800 US Hwy. 2 E, Columbia Falls, 406-892-1210
montanavortex.com

MEET THE FURRY RESIDENTS OF RED LODGE

Rescued animals in need of care find a safe and loving home at the Yellowstone Wildlife Sanctuary in Red Lodge. The sanctuary houses a range of animals from birds to mammals to reptiles.

Their goal is to only accept animals that are native to the Greater Yellowstone Ecosystem, thereby ensuring that all the residents are comfortable in their outdoor habitats.

Support these beautiful creatures by visiting the sanctuary to explore the grounds on your own, or for a special experience, sign up for a guided tour. Learn what makes the Greater Yellowstone Ecosystem unique and hear the heartwarming story of residents like Bob the bobcat, Dahlia the fox, Luna the bison, and Lurch the turkey vulture.

Combine the tour with an Animal Encounter for an up-close meeting with Piglet the hognose snake, or M&M the tiger salamander.

615 2nd St. E, Red Lodge, 406-446-1133
yellowstonewildlifesanctuary.org

BRUSH ACROSS
WESTERN ART WEEK

A flurry of talented artists from across Montana, and from across the country, descend upon Great Falls every spring in celebration of Western Art Week.

The event runs from Wednesday to Sunday around March 19, corresponding with the birthdate of Charlie Russell, Great Falls's beloved cowboy artist. Western Art Week has exploded in popularity since its inaugural event over 50 years ago.

More than 800 artists display their work at more than 15 shows in various locations around town, like Paris Gibson Square Museum of Art and the historic Hotel Arvon. The range of mediums is staggering, from watercolors, oil paintings, and sculptures to fine art photography and woodworking.

What ties all the artists together is their deep love of the people, landscapes, and wildlife of the West. Art lovers will relish the opportunity to chat with artists in person, watch them work, and purchase a unique piece to take home.

visitgreatfallsmontana.org/western-art-week

GREET THE ANIMALS
OF YELLOWSTONE

Forget battling the crowds in Yellowstone National Park for a remote chance of glimpsing grizzly bears, wolves, otters, and raptors. Simply make a stop at the Grizzly & Wolf Discovery Center in West Yellowstone.

This nonprofit wildlife sanctuary and education center is dedicated to caring for animals that are no longer able to live in the wild for various reasons.

The center also has numerous exhibits that teach visitors about the many animals that make their home in and around Montana, and what we can all do to help protect them.

Get a safe yet up-close view as massive grizzlies bound through their large outdoor habitat, swatting at trout in the pond and turning over rocks in the hunt for food hidden by the staff. Hear gray wolves howl and watch them play in the deep snow during the winter months.

201 S Canyon St., West Yellowstone, 406-646-7001
grizzlydiscoveryctr.org

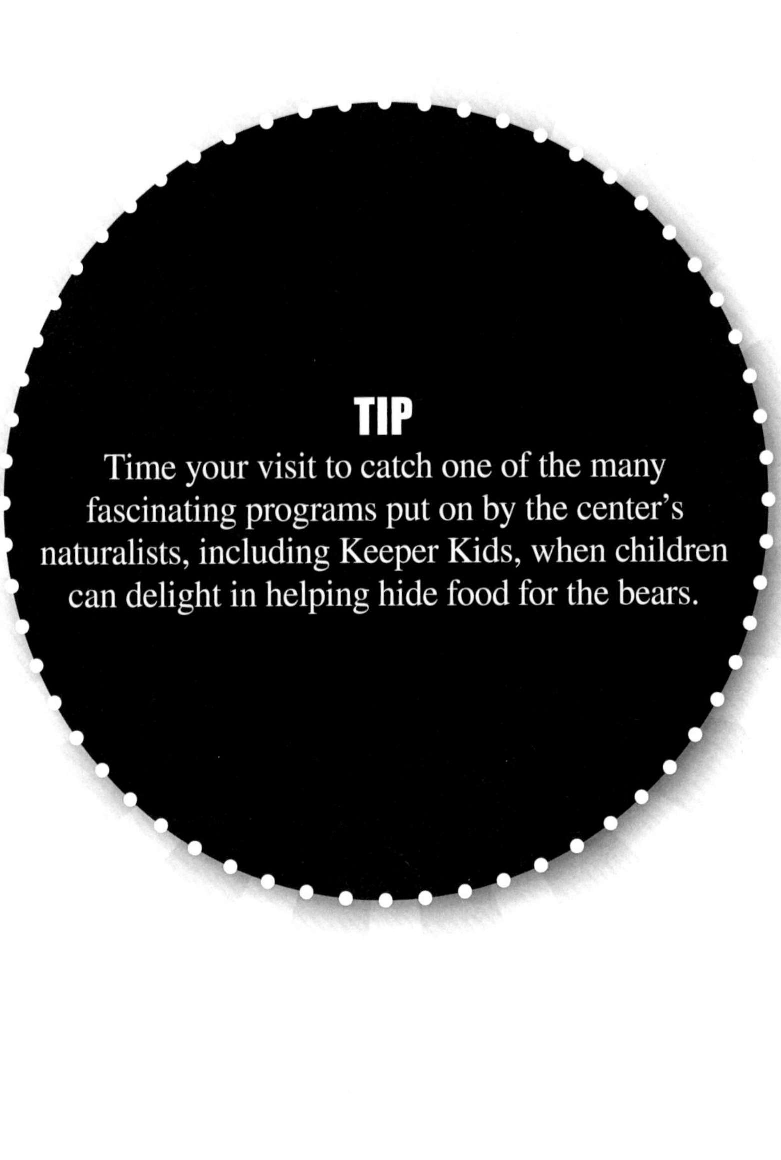

TIP

Time your visit to catch one of the many fascinating programs put on by the center's naturalists, including Keeper Kids, when children can delight in helping hide food for the bears.

KICK UP YOUR HEELS
AT MONTANA FOLK FESTIVAL

For many years, the National Folk Festival has been holding festivals in towns across the country in the hopes that the host communities will continue the tradition and create their own events. After hosting from 2008 to 2010, Butte's community organization, Mainstreet Uptown Butte, accepted the folk festival challenge and created the wildly successful Montana Folk Festival.

Boogie down at this entertaining event the second full weekend in July to hear musicians from around the country, and from around the world, play for enthusiastic crowds. The lineup changes each year. Past performers include Native American drum groups from Montana, Gaelic singers from Ireland, a Mexican American master fiddle player, Tennessee bluegrass bands, and a Ukrainian folk musician.

Throughout the three-day festival, fill up on barbecue, tamales, and ice cream from the wide variety of food vendors, and shop for traditional arts and crafts at the Montana Traditions Market.

PO Box 696, Butte, 406-497-6464
montanafolkfestival.com

TIP

All you have to do is show up. The festival is free and there is no need to purchase tickets. But if you plan on staying in or around Butte, book your lodging early as hotel rooms and campsites fill up fast.

OTHER MONTANA MUSIC FESTIVALS

Magic City Blues
308 6th Ave. N, Billings, 406-534-0400
magiccityblues.com

Rockin' the Rivers
1865 Montana Hwy. 2, Cardwell, 406-285-0099
rockintherivers.com

Hardtimes Bluegrass Festival
424 Forest Hill Rd., Hamilton, 406-821-3777
hardtimesbluegrass.com

Red Lodge Songwriter Festival
PO Box 830, Red Lodge, 406-690-5988
redlodgesongwriterfestival.org

Montana Baroque Music Festival
190 Montana Hwy. 135, Paradise, 406-826-3150
quinnshotsprings.com/baroque

Red Ants Pants Music Festival
206 E Main St., White Sulphur Springs, 406-209-8135
redantspantsmusicfestival.com

HOP ON

THE LAST CHANCE TOUR TRAIN

You could easily explore Helena's rich historical sites and bustling downtown on foot, but why not take it all in on a relaxing and informative ride aboard the Last Chance Tour Train.

Board one of the open-air train cars in front of the Montana Heritage Center adjacent to the state capitol. With no tracks to follow, the engineer is free to wander the streets while he regales you with tales of Helena's captivating, and sometimes wild, history.

Roll through the historic Mansion District past stately homes dating back to the late 1800s. Look for hitching posts that still line the streets where Helena's original citizens "parked" their rides.

The second part of the tour heads to Last Chance Gulch where you'll learn about Helena's thriving commerce yesterday and today, and current citizens offer up a friendly wave as you pass on by.

225 N Roberts St., Helena, 406-442-1023
lctours.com

TIP

Your boarding pass, which you receive when you check in for the tour, includes discounts and freebies at 12 shops, restaurants, and attractions throughout downtown. Plan to start your visit to Helena with the train ride so you can take advantage of these deals.

43

DRILL INTO
THE WORLD MUSEUM OF MINING

Prosperous mines full of silver and copper earned Butte the nickname "The Richest Hill on Earth." Make a visit to Butte's World Museum of Mining to learn about these boom days, and gain a new level of respect for the men who descended into the mines, risking their lives to make a living.

Above ground, explore the shops and offices of a re-created 1890s mining town and climb into the workings of a towering headframe. Be sure to sign up for the fascinating Underground Mine Tour.

Don your hard hat and headlamp as you follow your guide 100 feet below into the depths of the Orphan Girl Mine. Learn the fascinating yet laborious process of extracting precious metals from the hard rock walls.

Then, take a deep breath as you turn off your light and find out what it is like to be plunged into total darkness.

155 Museum Way, Butte, 406-723-7211
miningmuseum.org

Freezeout Lake

SPORTS AND RECREATION

44

EXPLORE THE BADLANDS
AT MAKOSHIKA STATE PARK

Makoshika State Park is tucked away on the eastern edge of the state just outside of Glendive, 40 miles from the North Dakota border.

Getting to Montana's largest state park may take some effort, but the natural wonders you'll discover there make the drive well worth it. The word Makoshika is a variation of the Lakota phrase meaning "bad land" or "bad earth," implying that it's a place to avoid.

Resist that implication and be rewarded with sweeping views of the surrounding landscape, towering colorful rock formations, and outcroppings of sweet-smelling juniper bushes. Stop at the visitor center to pick up a map, then drive the one main road that bisects the park.

To get a true feel for these badlands, lace up your boots and hike the rugged trails, keeping an eye out for golden eagles and turkey vultures circling above the cliffs.

1301 Snyder Ave., Glendive, 406-377-6256
fwp.mt.gov/makoshika

SOAK UP THE VIEWS
AT QUINN'S HOT SPRINGS

Quinn's Hot Springs Resort lies five miles outside the town of Paradise, and right in the center of true paradise. Find your perfect spot in one of the seven relaxing pools and take in views of the surrounding forest-draped mountains.

Temperatures of the spring-fed waters range from 90 to 106 degrees. Three of the pools are limited to ages 14 and over, and one pool is for adults only. For the best experience, book a room at the resort.

Options range from the adults-only Glacier Lodge to family cabins that overlook the Clark Fork River. All are within a short walk of the pools. Wristbands act as your room and locker key for a worry-free stay.

Dry off for a sumptuous meal at the on-site Harwood House restaurant. Throw your suit back on, grab a drink at the bar, and finish the evening soaking under the stars.

190 Montana Hwy. 135, Paradise, 406-826-3150, ext. 1
quinnshotsprings.com

TIP

Resort guests have unlimited access to the pools from 7 a.m. to 11 p.m. Anyone wishing to soak, but not stay, must make reservations through Quinn's website. Sessions are limited to four hours and cost $18.

ROAM WITH BUFFALO
AT THE BISON RANGE

Go back in time when herds of majestic bison covered the Montana landscape on a visit to the Bison Range.

This 18,000-acre swath of land located on the Flathead Indian Reservation in Moiese, formally known as the National Bison Range, has been managed by the Confederated Salish and Kootenai Tribes since 2020.

Check out the gift shop and informative museum at the visitor center. Then set off on the 19-mile Red Sleep Mountain Drive to see herds of bison and groups of pronghorn antelope on the rolling grasslands, elk in the river bottoms cloaked with cottonwoods, and maybe even a black bear trudging through the ponderosa pine forests.

You are required to stay in your vehicle throughout much of the range, but there is a lovely shaded picnic area just past the entrance and a few designated walking trails to stretch your legs.

58355 Bison Range Rd., Moiese, 406-644-2211
bisonrange.org

Red Sleep Mountain Drive is unpaved, one-way, and has steep descending switchbacks that tempt you to ride the brakes all the way down. Plus, the road is only open from May through October. It's stunning if you're up for it, but for a less intense and year-round alternative, take the level two-way Prairie Drive, which still offers abundant wildlife-watching opportunities.

47

HIKE THE 'ROOT

There are boundless opportunities to hit the trail in Montana, whether it be roaming the badlands of the eastern plains or weaving through alpine forests of the northwest.

For those looking to settle in for a while and explore several trails within a short distance of one another, there are few options better than the Bitterroot Valley. The Bitterroot Valley, known simply as "the 'Root" to locals, runs roughly 60 miles along US Highway 93 from Florence to Sula.

The valley is known for forested canyons, waterfalls, and jagged peaks. Warm up your legs outside of Darby with a level walk around Lake Como, the largest lake in the valley. Head over to Blodgett Canyon in Hamilton and make the gradual climb to the waterfall. When you're ready, trek 3.5 miles to the top of Saint Mary Peak looming 9,300 feet above Stevensville for spectacular views of the surrounding Bitterroot Mountains.

glaciermt.com/hiking

SKI
ACROSS WHITEFISH LAKE GOLF COURSE

If you've never tried cross-country skiing, or are just looking for a fun space to practice your moves, visit the Whitefish Lake Golf Course when the greens become blanketed with white.

Each winter, members of Whitefish's Glacier Nordic Club take over the golf course once the snow begins to fall, giving cross-country skiers of all abilities access to 12 kilometers, or 7.4 miles, of well-groomed trails. Visit the Glacier Nordic Center located on the golf course to purchase a day pass, then head out to ski the trails throughout the course.

Glide through the tunnel under Highway 93 to gain access to even more trails that weave through pine forests behind Grouse Mountain Lodge and past the shores of Loon Lake. Novice skiers can rent skis, boots, and poles at the center, and sign up for clinics to learn classic and skate skiing techniques from qualified instructors.

1200 US Hwy. 93, Whitefish, 406-862-9498
glaciernordicclub.org

RELAX
AT SLEEPING BUFFALO HOT SPRINGS

Hot springs in Montana run the gamut from high-end resorts to remote pools that can only be reached on foot. Sleeping Buffalo Hot Springs in Saco falls somewhere in between.

Located in the northeast corner of the state just off US Highway 2, Sleeping Buffalo provides inexpensive access to uncrowded and relaxing hot springs.

The water percolates from a 3,200-foot-deep artesian well first tapped in the 1920s by a man hoping to find oil, not water. Over time, these waters were used as a giant bathtub for cowboys and provided relief for a rancher's polio-stricken son, until the final incarnation as a health resort.

Find plenty of space in the large pool where the temperature resembles a comfortable hot tub. Serious soakers can move between the 106-degree and freezing plunge pools. The springs are fully enclosed with dark wood ceilings and rock walls that provide shelter from the windswept plains.

669 Buffalo Trl., Saco, 406-527-3320
sbhotsprings.com

TIP

Sleeping Buffalo also offers lodging, from deluxe cabins and suites to RV and tent sites. Purchase a few groceries and pool toys at the small store and enjoy a meal at the Buffalo Saloon.

OTHER MONTANA HOT SPRINGS

Fairmont Hot Springs Resort
1500 Fairmont Rd., Fairmont, 406-797-3241
fairmontmontana.com

Chico Hot Springs Resort & Day Spa
163 Chico Rd., Pray, 406-333-4933
chicohotsprings.com

Spa Hot Springs Motel
202 W Main St., White Sulphur Springs, 406-547-3366
spahotsprings.com

Yellowstone Hot Springs Resort
24 E Gate Rd., Gardiner, 406-848-4141
yellowstonehotspringsmt.com

Broadwater Hot Springs
4920 W US Hwy. 12, Helena, 406-443-5777
broadwatermt.com

Norris Hot Springs
42 Montana Hwy. 84, Norris, 406-685-3303
norrishotsprings.com

Boulder Hot Springs
31 Hot Springs Rd., Boulder, 406-225-4339
boulderhotsprings.com

Lolo Hot Springs
38500 W US Hwy. 12, Lolo, 406-273-2290
lolohotsprings.com

50

PLAY IN THE SNOW
AT GLACIER NATIONAL PARK

There's no doubt that Glacier National Park is a wondrous place to visit in the summer, but oh the crowds! For a truly unique experience, visit the park in the winter when most of the roads are closed to vehicles and the throngs of summer tourists have gone home.

You can enter the park on foot pretty much anywhere in the winter. You can also drive in at the West Glacier entrance and continue a short distance up Going-to-the-Sun Road to where the snowplows stop at the boarded-up Lake McDonald Lodge.

Park your car and start up the iconic road on foot, snowshoes, or cross-country skis, hoping for a glimpse of a moose tromping through the deep snow or an elusive pine marten flitting among the pine branches as you savor the quiet solitude of winter.

PO Box 128, West Glacier, 406-888-7800
nps.gov/glac

TIP

Be prepared to buy a park pass if you enter in a vehicle, even in the winter. Passes can be purchased at one of the entrance gates or on the park's website.

51

FLOAT YOUR CARES
DOWN THE MADISON RIVER

One of the best ways to cool off on a hot summer day is kicking back in an inner tube while drifting down a lazy Montana river.

The state has an abundance of rivers to get your float on, especially if you have your own tube and access to two cars for a shuttle between the put-in and take-out locations.

To ensure the logistics are someone else's worry, book a trip with Madison River Tubing in Bozeman. They supply you with a deluxe inner tube and transportation to and from the river. Your only chore is to relax and let the cool waters of the meandering Madison carry you through the wide river canyon.

Raise a toast to other floaters with cans of locally brewed Bozone Amber Ale that you just happened to pack and chill to perfection with a dunk in the river.

1110 W Main St., Bozeman, 406-209-8384
madisonrivertubing.com

52

MIGRATE
TO FREEZEOUT LAKE

Whether you're a dedicated bird-watcher or just starting out, the spring migration at Freezeout Lake Wildlife Management Area is truly a sight to behold.

From late March to early April, tens of thousands of snow geese flock to the ponds at the management area, located five miles outside of Fairfield off US Highway 89. The open water provides the perfect place for the migrating birds to rest, while the vast grain fields adjacent to the ponds provide the perfect place to refuel.

Witness this spectacle by driving along the gravel roads that surround the ponds. Park and get ready for the heart-stopping moment when thousands of geese swirl into the air as one, flying from the ponds to the grain fields and back. Breakfast liftoff is generally at sunrise, then the birds return to Freezeout until the late afternoon dinner flight commences.

PO Box 488, Fairfield, 406-467-2488
myfwp.mt.gov/fwppub/landsmgmt/sitedetail.action?lmsid=39753634

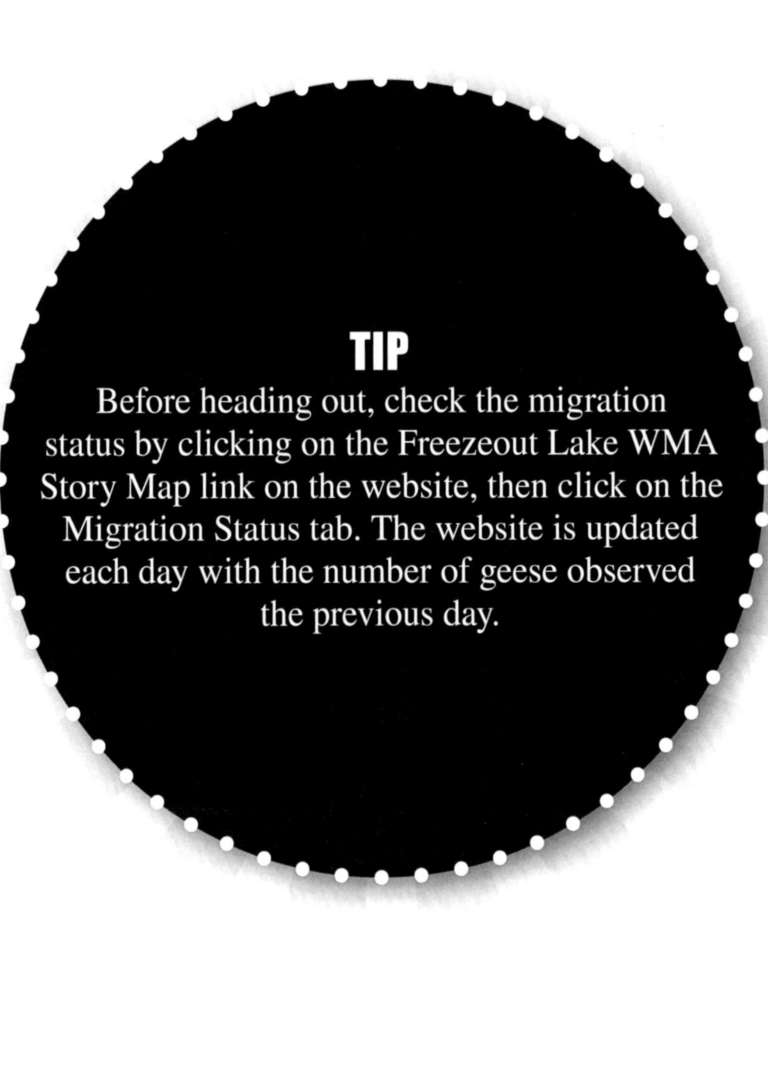
TIP
Before heading out, check the migration status by clicking on the Freezeout Lake WMA Story Map link on the website, then click on the Migration Status tab. The website is updated each day with the number of geese observed the previous day.

FLOCK
TO BOWDOIN NATIONAL WILDLIFE REFUGE

Spanning 15,550 acres of marsh, native short-grass prairie, and open water dotted with islands, Bowdoin National Wildlife Refuge is a bird-watcher's paradise.

The refuge attracts a staggering number of migratory and resident birds, and provides nesting habitat for many species of waterfowl and songbirds.

To best explore Bowdoin, take the 15-mile auto tour that begins at the refuge's headquarters, 7.5 miles east of Malta. Follow the one-way, very narrow gravel road as it encircles Lake Bowdoin and leads you through a range of prime bird habitat. Look for American white pelican, green-winged teal, and eared grebe swimming in the lake, and American avocet and marbled godwit along the shore.

Iridescent white-faced ibis high-step the ponds, stabbing the water with their curved bills in search of prey. Watch for sharp-tailed grouse scurrying into the tall cattails as you pass, and listen for common yellowthroat singing from the cottonwood trees.

194 Bowdoin Auto Tour Rd., Malta, 406-654-2863
fws.gov/refuge/bowdoin

OTHER BIRD-WATCHING HOT SPOTS IN MONTANA

Lee Metcalf National Wildlife Refuge
4567 Wildfowl Ln., Stevensville, 406-777-5552
fws.gov/refuge/lee-metcalf

Ninepipe National Wildlife Refuge
Junction of Montana Hwy. 212 and US Hwy. 93, Charlo, 406-750-8242
fws.gov/refuge/ninepipe

Benton Lake National Wildlife Refuge
922 Bootlegger Trail, Great Falls, 406-727-7400
fws.gov/refuge/benton-lake

Medicine Lake National Wildlife Refuge
223 N Shore Rd., Medicine Lake, 406-789-2305
fws.gov/refuge/medicine-lake

Lone Pine State Park
300 LonePine Rd., Kalispell, 406-755-2706
fwp.mt.gov/stateparks/lone-pine

Missouri Headwaters State Park
1585 Trident Rd., Three Forks, 406-285-3610
fwp.mt.gov/missouri-headwaters

Shiloh Conservation Area
1132 Shiloh Rd., Billings, 406-657-8433
billingsmtpublicworks.gov/258/shiloh-conservation-area

First Peoples Buffalo Jump

Bair Family Museum

Seeley–Swan Scenic Drive

C. M. Russell Museum

Wild Horse Island

Fort Benton

Lewis and Clark Interpretive Center

Gates of the Mountains Boat Tour

Bannack State Park

Daly Mansion

American Computer and Robotics Museum

MUSEUM OF

Museum of the Rockies

Quinn's Hot Springs Resort,
courtesy of Noah Couser Photography

Sacajawea Hotel

FLY-FISH
THE GALLATIN RIVER

One of the most iconic scenes in Montana is that of a lone figure standing ankle-deep in rippling clear waters, rhythmically casting a line through the air then whipping it back just as it kisses the surface.

You can be at the center of this fly-fishing scene in dozens of rivers and streams throughout the state, but few offer the guarantee of a bite like the canyons of the Gallatin River, just outside of Big Sky.

Experienced anglers can fish on their own, but those new to the sport will want the benefit of an experienced instructor from Gallatin River Guides. The friendly and knowledgeable guides will provide all the equipment you need, transport you to their favorite fishing holes in the shallow pools along the grassy shores, and patiently teach you all the techniques needed to land a shimmering rainbow trout.

47430 Gallatin Rd., Gallatin Gateway, 406-995-2290
montanaflyfishing.com

PADDLE

THE CLEARWATER CANOE TRAIL

Switch out your hiking boots and poles for sandals and paddles to get ready for a float down the Clearwater Canoe Trail.

The trail follows a lovely 3.5-mile stretch of the Clearwater River as it flows through the Lolo National Forest and into the blue waters of Seeley Lake.

Bring your own canoe, kayak, or paddleboard, or rent a canoe through Tamaracks Resort in the town of Seeley Lake. As part of the rental package, they will transport the boat to the trailhead and pick it up at the end.

Once on the water, settle in for a relaxing paddle as the river meanders through lush meadows bordered by pine forests. Listen for the haunting calls of loons and watch for deer and moose along the riverbank. Once at the lake, follow the level one-mile hiking trail that parallels the river to get back to the trailhead.

Tamaracks Resort
3481 Montana Hwy. 83 N, Seeley Lake, 406-677-2433
tamaracks.com

Seeley Lake Ranger District
3583 Montana Hwy. 83 N, Seeley Lake, 406-677-2233
fs.usda.gov/recarea/lolo/recreation/recarea/?recid=10327&actid=43

CRUISE
TO WILD HORSE ISLAND

The deep waters of Flathead Lake that surround Wild Horse Island offer refuge to the small herd of resident wild horses that give the island its name, along with bighorn sheep, mule deer, and bald eagles.

You can access this enchanting island by boat, but dock space is limited and it can take an hour of kayaking through often choppy waters to get there. For a carefree visit, sign up for a shuttle with Big Arm Boat Rentals and Rides.

The shuttle runs three times a day from May through early September. At 2,100 acres, chances of seeing the namesake stallions are slim, but there are so many other fun things to do. Explore the shoreline on the Skeeko Bay Trail, climb to the highest point for breathtaking views of Flathead Lake and the Mission Mountains, or simply lounge on the beach watching the boats sail by.

Big Arm Boat Rentals and Rides
44227 A St., Big Arm, 406-260-5090
boatrentalsandrides.com

Flathead Lake State Park—Wild Horse Island
Unit 8600, Montana Hwy. 35, Bigfork, 406-837-3041
fwp.mt.gov/wild-horse-island

57

RAFT
THROUGH THE ALBERTON GORGE

"All paddle," your guide cries, signaling that it's time for your arms and heart to start pumping in sync before your raft plunges through the rapids. Few experiences in the Montana outdoors are quite as exhilarating as whitewater rafting.

To experience this exhilaration under the protection of an experienced guide, book a 12-mile trip through the Alberton Gorge of the Clark Fork River with Lewis & Clark Trail Adventures in Missoula.

Water pounds through the canyons of the Clark Fork in the height of summer resulting in class II and III rapids, safe enough for novice paddlers yet wild enough to guarantee thrills. Lewis & Clark provides everything you need for a safe yet exciting ride. Buck through rapids with descriptive names like "Tumbleweed" and "Fang," then end the journey with a hop in the river as it calms to soothe your tired arms.

912 E Broadway Ave., Missoula, 406-728-7609
trailadventures.com

58

SWING
ACROSS THE KOOTENAI RIVER

Twelve miles west of Libby, the mighty Kootenai River crashes over a 30-foot-high waterfall that strikes fear in the hearts of the most accomplished, and foolhardy, paddlers.

It is here where Meryl Streep rowed for her life in the movie *The River Wild*, and Leonardo DiCaprio was swept away in *The Revenant*. You can experience amazing views of this stunning river gorge without the magic of movies by crossing the Kootenai Falls Swinging Bridge.

To get to the bridge, park in the lot at Mile Marker 21 along US Highway 2, then follow the half-mile trail. Despite the name, this suspension bridge is quite safe, although crossing it does provide a thrill as you walk, and sway, across its 220-foot span. Take a deep breath and pause in the middle to take in the rushing river below as it churns past the rugged cliffs.

Kootenai National Forest Office
31374 US Hwy. 2, Libby, 406-293-6211
fs.usda.gov/detailfull/kootenai/specialplaces/?cid=fseprd1008852

TIP

The first 500 feet of the trail is handicapped accessible and leads to an overlook of the falls. The remainder of the trail is rocky, somewhat steep, and requires climbing a metal stairway to a railroad overpass.

Kootenai Falls Swinging Bridge

RAMBLE AMONG
THE GIANTS OF ROSS CREEK

Ancient and colossal western red cedar trees are the star attraction at Ross Creek Cedars Scenic Area, 25 miles south of Troy in the shadow of the remote Cabinet Mountains.

Explore this forest sanctuary by following the dirt-covered nature trail that loops through the grove past cedar trees, some close to 1,000 years old, as well as grand fir, western white pine, and Engelmann spruce.

The rich smell of cedar fills the air as you cross the bridge over Ross Creek. Be prepared to give your neck a workout craning to see the treetops 175 feet overhead. Make a vain attempt to wrap your arms around trunks spanning over 12 feet in diameter. Interpretive signs along the loop tell the history of this area and identify what other plants and animals you may see and hear, like scurrying chipmunks and the distant drumming of a pileated woodpecker.

Kootenai National Forest Office
31374 US Hwy. 2, Libby, 406-293-6211
fs.usda.gov/recarea/kootenai/recarea/?recid=66084

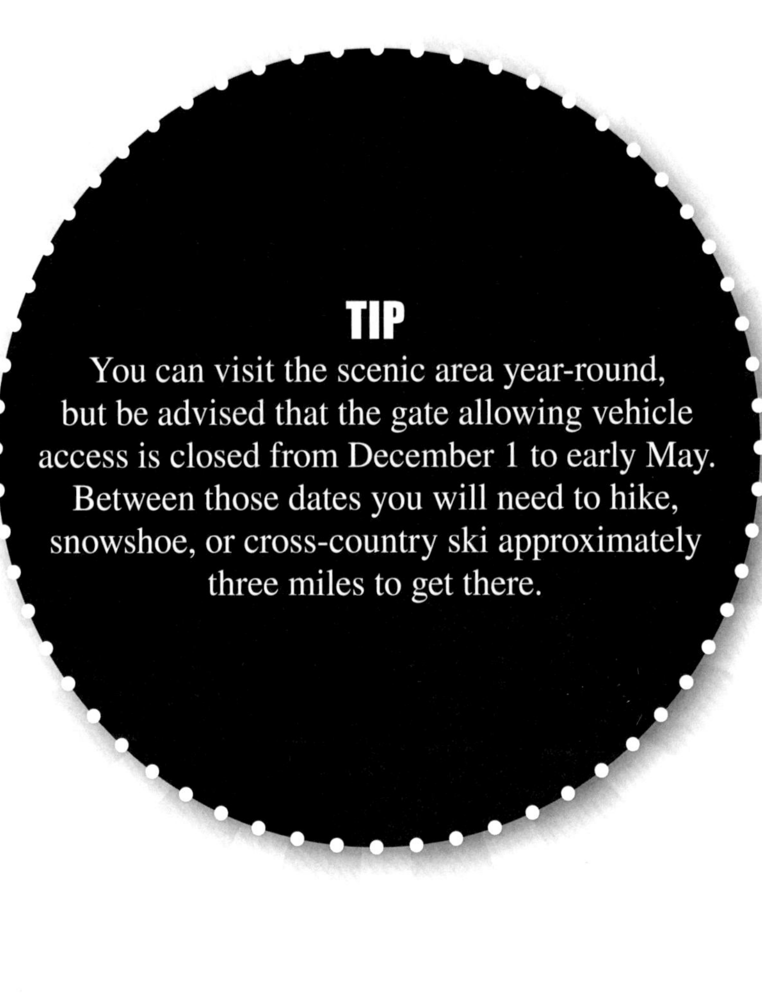

TIP

You can visit the scenic area year-round, but be advised that the gate allowing vehicle access is closed from December 1 to early May. Between those dates you will need to hike, snowshoe, or cross-country ski approximately three miles to get there.

60

SUMMER ON THE SLOPES
IN WHITEFISH

Whitefish Mountain Resort offers exciting adventures on its ski slopes long after the white stuff has melted. Ride the ski lift over 2,000 vertical feet up the mountain, then race down more than 25 miles of mountain bike trails.

Thrill seekers will love Montana's longest zip-line tour. Take the lift, then hike from station to station where you'll be strapped into a secure harness to fly across 1,900 feet of line suspended 300 feet above the treetops.

Looking for fun with a little less excitement? Ride a sled down the twists and turns of the alpine slide. Travel tree to tree by swing and rope bridges at the Aerial Adventure Park, or simply take in the views at your own pace on the hiking trails.

Other ski resorts that offer summer activities can be found at Big Sky Resort and Missoula's Snowbowl.

Whitefish Mountain Resort
1015 Glades Dr., Whitefish, 406-862-2900
skiwhitefish.com

Big Sky Resort
50 Big Sky Resort Rd., Big Sky, 406-995-5749
bigskyresort.com

Snowbowl
1700 Snowbowl Rd., Missoula, 406-549-9777
montanasnowbowl.com

61

SHINE A LIGHT
ON LEWIS AND CLARK CAVERNS

Explore one of the largest limestone caves in North America at Lewis and Clark Caverns State Park, 18 miles east of Whitehall.

Entry into the caverns is only allowed on guided tours that run from May through September. Choose from tours based on your level of comfort and adventure.

The Paradise Tour grants those with limited mobility and families with small children access to the largest and most ornate room in the cave.

Looking for more adventure? Journey deeper into the cave on the Classic Cave Tour, which requires walking two miles and up and down 600 stairs as you duck under rock ledges past dripping stalactites. Channel one of the first explorers of the cave during the Candlelight Cave Tours in December, when each spelunker is given a candle lantern to light their way. Just don't let it blow out!

25 Lewis and Clark Caverns Rd., Whitehall, 406-287-3541
fwp.mt.gov/stateparks/lewis-and-clark-caverns

TIP

Tickets for the Candlelight Cave Tours go fast. Begin checking the website in September so you don't miss out.

FOLLOW
THE RIVER'S EDGE TRAIL

Walk, bike, or run past the canyons and falls of the Missouri River as it flows through Great Falls on the River's Edge Trail.

A recreationist's dream, the trail consists of paved, dirt, and gravel trails that extend along both sides of the river for almost 60 miles.

Start the trail in the heart of Great Falls, or take advantage of the many parking areas along the way to explore sections. Stroll along the 3.5-mile Urban Loop to admire public artwork and watch for American pelicans coming in for a landing on Sacajawea Island. Expert mountain bikers will enjoy the wild turns on the Mayhem Trails as they hug the river canyon walls.

See amazing views of Black Eagle Falls from the 2.1-mile Giant Springs Loop, and visit Giant Spring State Park, home to one the largest freshwater springs in the world, and the Roe, the world's shortest river.

PO Box 553, Great Falls
thetrail.org

63

VOYAGE THROUGH GATES OF THE MOUNTAINS

The boat tour through the Gates of the Mountains is an experience not to be missed. Board the open-air boat at the marina, 20 miles north of Helena, for a cruise through a breathtaking section of the Missouri River surrounded by towering limestone cliffs.

During the two-hour cruise, your captain will steer the boat through the river while talking about the history and geology of the area, pointing out dark caves that cut deep into the rock and slowing for sightings of bald eagles circling overhead.

Take a moment to reflect on the long line of people who have plied these waters before you.

Meriwether Lewis first documented this stretch of the river, but look to the pictographs high on the cliff walls as evidence that this area was used as a byway centuries before the Corps of Discovery's famous expedition.

3131 Gates of the Mountains Rd., Helena, 406-458-5241
gatesofthemountains.com

DRIVE
THE SEELEY–SWAN

You can throw a dart pretty much anywhere on a map of Montana and hit a scenic roadway, but few tick all the boxes for a lovely day on the road like the Seeley–Swan Valley.

This scenic drive follows Montana Highway 83 north for 90 miles until spilling out at Bigfork. Gas up the car and load up on snacks since you'll find few towns along the stretch, but that's just fine.

What you will find are stunning views of the towering Mission Mountains to the west and the remote, rugged Swan Mountains to the east. Dozens of shimmering lakes reflect the mountain peaks, and moose feed in the willow ponds.

Opportunities to stop and explore are in abundance, like at the Swan River National Wildlife Refuge. Watch for mule deer bounding through the meadow and listen for the winnowing call of Wilson's snipe.

visitmt.com/listings/general/scenic-highway/seeleyswan-scenic-drive

TIP
To begin the drive, follow Montana Highway 200 west from Missoula for 38 miles to the turnoff onto Montana Highway 83 at Clearwater Junction. If you pass the giant cow, you've gone too far.

Little Bighorn Battlefield

CULTURE AND HISTORY

65

GO BELOW HAVRE
BENEATH THE STREETS

A devastating fire raged through the town of Havre on one eventful night in 1904, burning many businesses to the ground.

Rumor has it that the fire was set by a couple of men as revenge for being kicked out of a bar. Instead of giving up and moving on, many merchants went a different way and set up shop in the tunnels beneath the sidewalks until the town could be rebuilt.

You can take a tour of this re-created subterranean town today through Havre Beneath the Streets. Your tour guide will lead you through Boone's Drug Store, Wright's Dentist Office, and the Holland & Bonine Mortuary while explaining the history of each room.

Hand-cranked washing machines sit in Wah Ming's Laundry, giant ovens line the walls of Gourley Brothers Bakery, and partially drawn curtains offer some privacy for the beds in the bordello.

120 3rd Ave., Havre, 406-265-8888
havrebeneaththestreets.com

REST UP
AT SACAJAWEA HOTEL

History and luxury combine at the Sacajawea Hotel in Three Forks. Opened in 1910 as a stop for wealthy travelers coming into town along the Milwaukee Railroad, the "Sac," as it's affectionately known by the locals, suffered a series of ups and downs over the years.

In 2009, the Folkvord family, owners of Three Forks–based Wheat Montana Bakery, purchased the hotel and restored the Sac to its former glory.

Book a room today and enjoy a complimentary glass of champagne before checking into your comfy room with modern amenities. Relax in the lobby adorned with dark wood beams and an intricately decorated ceiling before moving outside to secure a seat on the enormous front porch.

In the evening, enjoy a hearty meal at Pompey's Grill, then head downstairs to rub elbows with the locals over a Montana-brewed beer at the Sac Bar.

5 N Main St., Three Forks, 406-285-6515
sacajaweahotel.com

LEARN THE HISTORY

BEHIND THE BATTLE OF LITTLE BIGHORN

On June 25, 1876, General George Armstrong Custer and 600 soldiers, civilians, and Indian scouts fought to win a losing battle against 2,000 Lakota, Cheyenne, and Arapahoe warriors at the Battle of Little Bighorn. This epic clash marked one of the last victories by the Northern Plains Indians as they fought against the US government to preserve their way of life. The battle is forever commemorated at the Little Bighorn Battlefield National Monument, 16 miles southeast of Hardin.

Begin at the visitor center to view artifacts from the battlefield, and listen as dedicated park rangers carefully detail the battle timeline. Stand on the somber Last Stand Hill to see where Custer and 41 of his men fell.

Tour the battlefield on the 10-mile Battlefield Road, and look out over the hills dotted with red and white gravestones marking where men fighting for both sides met their end.

756 Battlefield Tour Rd., Crow Agency, 406-638-3236
nps.gov/libi

TIP

To hear the Native American perspective of the battle, sign up for the Apsáalooke Tour given by the Crow Nation Office of Tourism. Tours run throughout the day, and tickets are sold in the gift shop inside the battlefield visitor center.

OTHER MONTANA BATTLEFIELDS

Big Hole National Battlefield
16425 Montana Hwy. 43 W, Wisdom, 406-689-3155
nps.gov/biho/index.htm

Bear Paw Battlefield
Route 240, Chinook, 406-357-3130
nps.gov/nepe/planyourvisit/visit-bear-paw-battlefield.htm

Rosebud Battlefield State Park
HC 42, Box 642, Busby, 406-757-2298
fwp.mt.gov/stateparks/rosebud-battlefield

WALK IN THE FOOTSTEPS
OF LEWIS AND CLARK

History buffs won't want to miss a visit to Travelers' Rest State Park in Lolo to see the only archaeologically verified campsite of the Lewis and Clark Expedition in the nation.

Browse the museum to see exhibits on both the Corps of Discovery and the history of the Salish people and other Native Americans who have called this area home for centuries. Move outside to follow the Main Loop Trail as it encircles the historic campsite.

Interpretive signs explain the historical significance of Travelers' Rest and provide details about the expedition's time here. The park is fortunate to have many dedicated volunteers who are eager to share their wealth of Lewis and Clark knowledge.

All you have to do is ask. Explore the rest of the 65-acre park on the two nature trails that grant access to Lolo Creek, a perfect place to go fishing or swimming on hot days.

6717 US Hwy. 12 W, Lolo, 406-273-4253
fwp.mt.gov/stateparks/travelers-rest

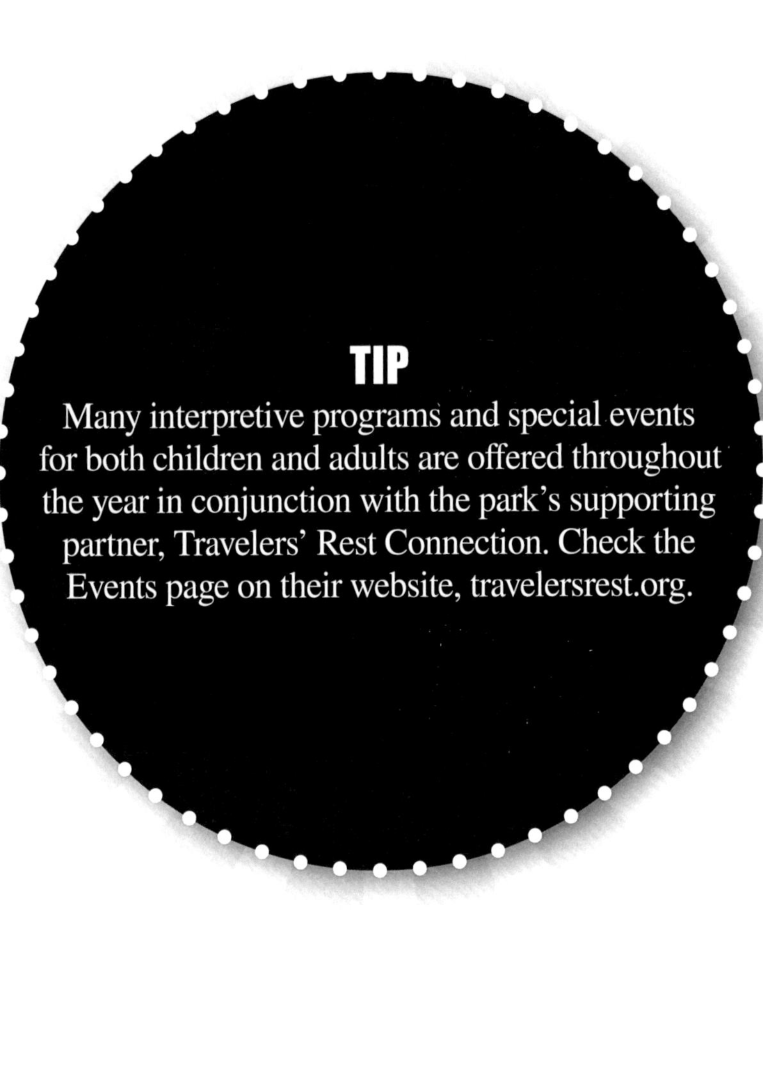

TIP

Many interpretive programs and special events for both children and adults are offered throughout the year in conjunction with the park's supporting partner, Travelers' Rest Connection. Check the Events page on their website, travelersrest.org.

69

ADMIRE THE ART OF THE FOREST

AT SCULPTURE IN THE WILD

Stunning works of art weave through the sun-dappled woods just north of Lincoln at Blackfoot Pathways: Sculpture in the Wild International Sculpture Park.

Since its inception in 2014, this outdoor art extravaganza has invited world-renowned sculptors to create unique installations that pay homage to the Blackfoot Valley's heritage with a focus on industry, culture, and the environment.

Take the dirt path as it leads you past more than 14 large-scale sculptures that use both natural and industrial materials to create fanciful and thought-provoking pieces. Twigs intertwine to form a house perfect for a hobbit in *Tree Circus* by Patrick Dougherty.

Fifteen tons of newspapers compress to create Steven Siegel's *Hill and Valley*. A swirl of logs draws you into *Ponderosa Whirlpool* by Chris Drury. Visit the park throughout the year to see how the sculptures change with the light and the seasons.

1500 E Montana Hwy. 200, Lincoln, 406-431-0325
sculptureinthewild.com

DRAW
INTO PICTOGRAPH CAVE STATE PARK

Let your eyes adjust to the light as you stand before Pictograph Cave. Watch as the faded red lines high on the cave wall slowly transform into works of art created by native peoples who sheltered under these sandstone eaves many years ago.

Seven miles outside Billings, Pictograph Cave State Park encompasses three caves: Pictograph, Middle, and Ghost. Pictograph is the only cave with drawings, but each one has its own unique beauty. Before setting off on the .75-mile loop that passes each cave, stop at the visitor center to learn about this wondrous site.

A steep but short climb takes you first to Pictograph Cave where red pigment images depicting animals and ceremonies dating back 2,000 years sit next to drawings of rifles done within the last 200 years. The images can be seen with the naked eye, but pack a pair of binoculars for the best view.

3401 Coburn Rd., Billings, 406-254-7342
fwp.mt.gov/stateparks/pictograph-cave

71

ROUND 'EM UP
AT GRANT-KOHRS RANCH

After purchasing a cattle ranch from Johnny Grant in 1866, Conrad Kohrs, the Cattle King of Montana, went on to spend the next 50 years of his life building a fortune here in the shadow of the Flint Creek Range.

Visit this working cattle ranch today at the Grant-Kohrs Ranch National Historic Site in Deer Lodge. Take a guided tour of the Kohrs family's 9,000-square-foot mansion and hear how Conrad's wife, Augusta, turned this bug-ridden man cave into an opulent home full of fine treasures from around the world.

Tours are offered year-round several times a day. Move on to explore other buildings on the property like the blacksmith shop, carriage house, and bunkhouse row. Interpretive signs detail interesting facts about the daily lives of cowboys who were vital in making the ranch a success. Rule number one for these cowpokes: weekly baths are required.

251 Grant Cir., Deer Lodge, 406-846-2070
nps.gov/grko

TIP
Check the ranch's Facebook page for special events from summer activities for the kids to ranching demonstrations at facebook.com/grantkohrsnhs.

72

TAKE A TOUR
OF OLD BUTTE

The Butte–Anaconda Historic District is one of the largest National Historic Landmark Districts in the nation, and many of those historic buildings are clustered in Uptown Butte—dubbed "Uptown" because you must climb a hill to reach it.

For an entertaining trip back in time to learn about Uptown Butte's rough-and-tumble legacy, sign up for a tour with Old Butte Historical Adventures.

Your guide will lead you through the city streets regaling you with tales of hard-working, hard-playing miners; wealthy Copper Kings; and ladies of the night who served them all.

Enter rooms closed off from the public for decades like the Rookwood Speakeasy with its two-way mirror used to screen patrons during the height of Prohibition.

The subterranean jail cells are a highlight of the tour where men and women—like Butte's native son, Evel Knievel—carved their names into the walls of the windowless cells.

117 N Main St., Butte, 406-498-3424
buttetour.info

OTHER GUIDED HISTORIC WALKING TOURS AROUND MONTANA

Western Heritage Center

2822 Montana Ave., Billings, 406-256-6809

ywhc.org

Unseen Missoula

218 E Main St., Ste. C, Missoula, 406-543-4238

missouladowntown.com/unseen-missoula

The Extreme History Project

234 E Mendenhall St., Bozeman, 406-220-2678

extremehistoryproject.org

Helena History Tours

1750 Washington St., Helena, 406-603-4916

mthistory.org/tours

73

DIG IN
AT MONTANA DINOSAUR CENTER

Watch out! That rock you're about to step on just might be a dinosaur bone. Not sure how to tell the difference? Sign up for an expedition with the Montana Dinosaur Center in Bynum, just one of the 14 stops on the Montana Dinosaur Trail.

The center lies atop the Two Medicine Formation where dinosaurs roamed 70.5 to 80.5 million years ago, and where their bones are now scattered across the badlands of the Rocky Mountain Front.

On the half-day fossil dig site tour, experienced guides help you spot Hadrosaur ribs, vertebrae, and femurs poking out from the dusty ground, and challenge you to a game to see who can find the most Maiasaura eggshell fragments.

Die-hard dino fans will geek out on the full-day dig expeditions as they learn the basics of fossil science and field mapping while helping to dig for dinosaurs at an active fossil site.

Montana Dinosaur Center
120 2nd Ave. S, Bynum, 406-469-2211
tmdinosaurcenter.org

Montana Dinosaur Trail
mtdinotrail.org

74

VIEW THE ART
OF CHARLIE RUSSELL

Many artists over the years have tried their hand at painting the American West, but few have perfectly captured its essence like Charles Marion Russell. After moving to Montana in 1880, Charlie went on to create approximately 4,000 works of art depicting scenes true to his life as a cowboy, from the brutality of winter to the daily grind of a cattle drive to respectful depictions of Native Americans before the onslaught of White settlers.

Charlie and his wife, Nancy, eventually moved to Great Falls where you can see an impressive collection of his work and tour his home and studio at the C. M. Russell Museum. Wander the galleries to admire close to 1,000 original Russell paintings and sculptures.

Great treasures of the museum are the letters he wrote to his many friends that show off his cheeky sense of humor in both words and illustrations.

400 13th St. N, Great Falls, 406-727-8787
cmrussell.org

EXPERIENCE NATIVE CULTURE
AT KYIYO POW WOW

Deep resounding drumbeats followed by drummers' high-pitched songs mark the start of the Grand Entrance at the Kyiyo Pow Wow.

Dancers of all ages cloaked in traditional dress slowly make their way into the arena. Men whirl, stomp, and bob their feathered headdresses. Women draped in magnificent beadwork slowly step to the drums.

Attending a Native American powwow is one of the most moving experiences you can have in Montana. The annual powwow put on by the Kyiyo Native American Student Association at the University of Montana in Missoula is one of the best places to take in this experience.

The April event welcomes tribes from across Montana, and from across the nation, to celebrate and share their cultures and traditions through song and dance. Be sure not to miss the Grand Entrance, then stay to watch the dancing and drumming contests.

32 Campus Dr., Missoula, 406-243-5946
umt.edu/kyiyo/kyiyopowwow

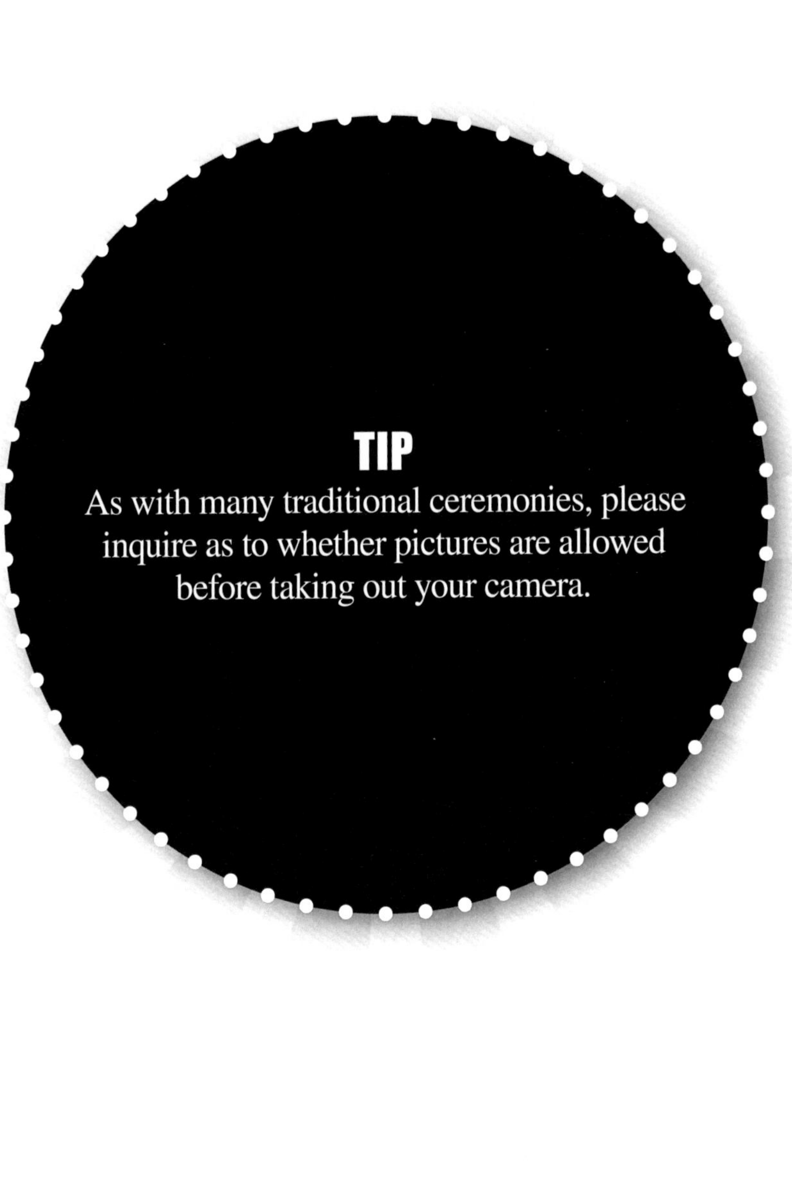

TIP

As with many traditional ceremonies, please inquire as to whether pictures are allowed before taking out your camera.

76

VISIT MUSEUM
OF THE ROCKIES

Discover one of the most extensive collections of fossils in the world at the Museum of the Rockies in Bozeman. The crown jewel of the museum is the Siebel Dinosaur Complex where these amazing fossils, many of which were dug up right here in Montana, are on display.

Marvel at Triceratops and mammoth skulls, dinosaur eggs, and Big Al, a nearly complete set of Allosaurus bones. Observe as the museum's resident paleontologists tend to recently uncovered fossils in the lab. Walk under one of the nation's few mounted Tyrannosaurus rex skeletons looming over it all.

Other exhibits educate visitors on the history of Yellowstone National Park and Native American cultures in Montana, yesterday and today. Get comfy in the planetarium as your seat reclines and the cosmos swirl overhead. Move outside to the Living History Farm and learn about life on a Montana homestead.

600 W Kagy Blvd., Bozeman, 406-994-2251
museumoftherockies.org

STAKE YOUR CLAIM
AT VIRGINIA CITY

Part museum, part tourist attraction, Virginia City has been frozen in time so you can experience what life was like in Montana's second territorial capital during the gold rush of 1865.

Stroll the boardwalks along Wallace Street visiting establishments much as they were back then, like the Bale of Hay Saloon, Montana's oldest watering hole. Step into the life-size dioramas to see fashions of the day at Kramer Dress Shop and rows of elixirs at Rank's Drugs.

Tour town aboard a stagecoach while listening to tales of Virginia City's infamous gang of vigilantes. Boo the villains and applaud the heroes during a performance at the Virginia City Players. Hop aboard the Alder Gulch Shortline Railroad for a trip to Virginia City's sister town, Nevada City. While there, chat with 1860s reenactors at the Nevada City Living History Museum and Music Hall.

300 ½ W Wallace St., Virginia City, 406-843-5247
virginiacitymt.com

SERVE TIME
AT OLD MONTANA PRISON

The Montana Territory was the epitome of the Wild West when the state's first prison was built in Deer Lodge in 1871. Take a fascinating self-guided tour at the Old Montana Prison & Auto Museum Complex to delve into the daily life of prisoners who served time within these imposing walls. Proceed with caution into the dank windowless cells of solitary West Siberia.

Learn about the devastating riot of 1959 that resulted in the murder of Deputy Warden Ted Rothe, and look for damage from the bazooka fired by the National Guard in the red brick tower of the Cell House.

The admission price also includes five other museums including Yesterday's Playthings doll and toy museum, the Powell County Museum, and the Montana Auto Museum, packed with more than 160 cars from an 1886 Benz to cherry-red muscle cars from the 1970s.

1106 Main St., Deer Lodge, 406-846-3111
pcmaf.org

TIP

If you dare, spend the night in the spooky prison on a Ghost Tour. Armed with paranormal investigation equipment, you'll be given access to parts of the prison closed to the public, like the hospital and death tower.

Old Montana Prison

TRAVEL BACK IN TIME
AT BANNACK STATE PARK

Ghosts of Montana's past swirl around as you walk down the dusty street of Bannack State Park. The discovery of gold in a nearby creek in 1862 resulted in the first mining claim filed in Montana. The rush was soon on and Bannack became Montana's first territorial capital, home to 3,000 families, politicians, and outlaws.

Start your tour of one of the state's best-preserved ghost towns at the visitor center to grab a map and learn the history of Bannack in the small museum. Then walk down Main Street to explore more than 50 preserved log and brick buildings. Review the day's lessons on the blackboard of the schoolhouse.

See remnants of a once-bubbling still at the Bootlegger Cabin, and plan your escape as the sheriff closes in. Climb the steep hill to the cemetery where Bannack's prominent citizens continue to oversee town to this very day.

721 Bannack Rd., Dillon, 406-834-3413
fwp.mt.gov/stateparks/bannack-state-park

OTHER MONTANA GHOST TOWNS

Garnet Ghost Town

PO Box 18295, Missoula, 406-329-3914

garnetghosttown.org

Granite Ghost Town State Park

347 Granite Rd., Philipsburg, 406-224-0833

fwp.mt.gov/stateparks/granite-ghost-town

Elkhorn State Park

812 Elkhorn St., Elkhorn, 406-577-7894

fwp.mt.gov/stateparks/elkhorn

Marysville

visitmt.com/listings/general/ghost-town/marysville

82

TRAVERSE THE GREAT FALLS
WITH THE CORPS OF DISCOVERY

The great falls of the Missouri River were pivotal to the Lewis and Clark Expedition. Not only did the falls signify the midway point on the men's, and one woman's, path to the Pacific Ocean, but it also proved to be their biggest challenge as they lugged boats and equipment along 18 miles of prairie to bypass the formidable falls.

The Lewis and Clark Interpretive Center in Great Falls chronicles this grueling portage, as well as the entire expedition from 1804 to 1806. The falls no longer hold their historic power due to a series of dams, but as you gaze out the window to the river today, you still get a sense of the expedition's enormous task.

Through detailed exhibits, artifacts, films, and ranger talks, you'll learn about the Native American tribes the expedition encountered and the many hardships they endured, from debilitating sickness to the fierce grizzly bear.

4201 Giant Springs Rd., Great Falls, 406-453-6248
fs.usda.gov/recarea/hlcnf/recarea/?recid=61458

STROLL THROUGH HISTORY
AT FORT BENTON

Fort Benton was established as a fur trading post in 1846 and is considered the birthplace of Montana.

With its proximity to the Canadian border, as the last stop for steamboats on the Missouri River, and with the absence of law enforcement, Fort Benton was also the perfect place for whiskey trading, bar fights, brothels, and anyone looking to make their fortune by nefarious means.

Discover Fort Benton's fascinating history by taking a walk along the Levee Trail. Read about the Bloodiest Block in the West; see the *Baby Rose*, one of the last steamboats on the river; and stand above the mighty Missouri on the Old Fort Benton Bridge. Cross the street to the Museum and Heritage Complex consisting of five museums like Old Fort Benton and the Museum of the Northern Great Plains. Reward your tired feet with a relaxing stay at the historic Grand Union Hotel.

PO Box 12, Fort Benton, 406-622-3864
fortbentonchamber.org/visitors

GIVE A SALUTE
TO FORT MISSOULA

Fort Missoula was constructed as a military post in its namesake town in 1877. Over the years, it served as regional headquarters for the Civilian Conservation Corps and an alien detention center for Italian and Japanese men during World War II until becoming the Historical Museum at Fort Missoula in 1975.

Start your visit at the 1911 Quartermaster's Storehouse Building where exhibits detail the history of the fort, the town of Missoula, and the fascinating history of the all African American 25th Infantry Bicycle Corps, made up of enlisted men who rode from Fort Missoula to Yellowstone National Park and even St. Louis in the late 1800s.

Move outside to explore the many buildings and other exhibits scattered on the grounds, including a 1907 one-room schoolhouse and trolley barn. Climb up into a 1930s fire lookout at the Forestry Interpretive Center and read the heartbreaking stories inside the Alien Detention Center Barracks.

3400 Captain Rawn Way, Missoula, 406-728-3476
fortmissoulamuseum.org

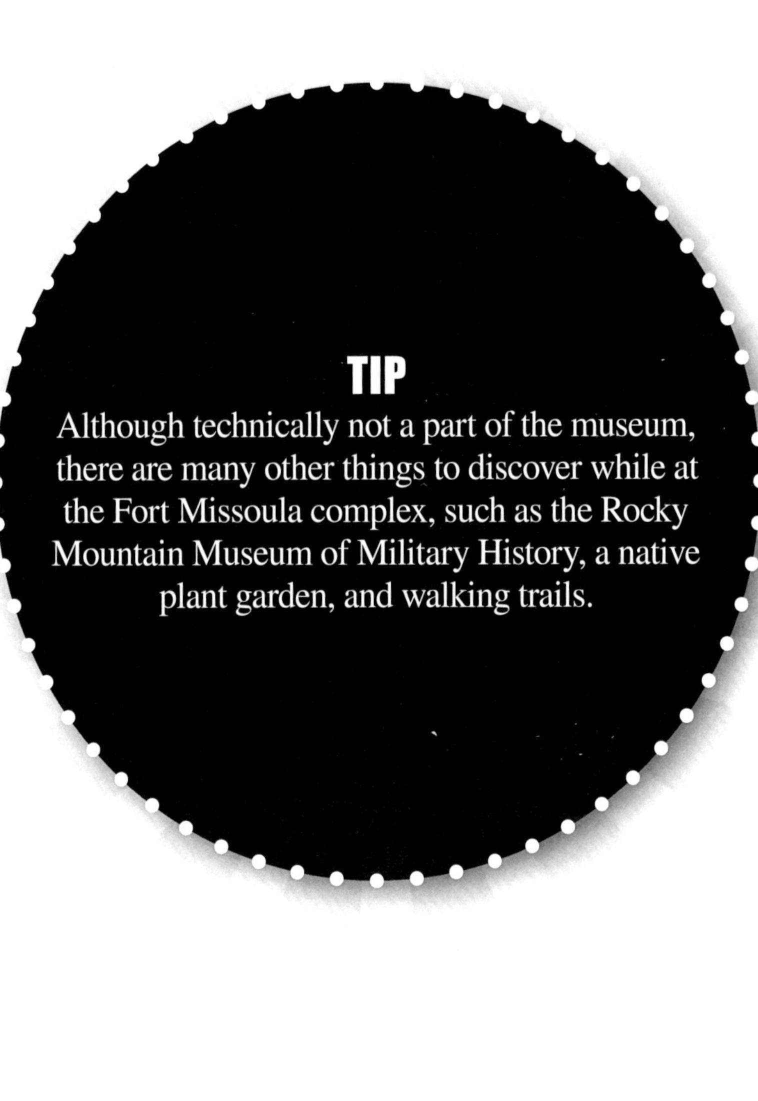
TIP
Although technically not a part of the museum, there are many other things to discover while at the Fort Missoula complex, such as the Rocky Mountain Museum of Military History, a native plant garden, and walking trails.

85

DISCOVER
THE BAIR FAMILY MUSEUM

The Charles M. Bair Family Museum is an unexpected delight on the rolling plains of central Montana. The patriarch of the Bair family, Charles, became wealthy during the Alaskan gold rush before turning his attention to ranching, becoming the owner of one of the largest sheep ranches in the world.

In the early 1900s, Charles and his wife, Mary, purchased a ranch in Martinsdale, and they, along with their two daughters, Marguerite and Alberta, set about decorating the home with an astonishing collection of Western, Native American, and European art.

Browse the museum to see paintings by Joseph H. Sharp and Native American beadwork and rugs. A dedicated docent will take you on a tour of the lovely grounds and the magnificent yet comfy Bair Family House. Marvel at treasures that adorn each room, including George III sterling silver, 17th-century furniture, and paintings by French and British masters.

2751 Montana Hwy. 294, Martinsdale, 406-572-3314
bairfamilymuseum.org

STAND AT THE EDGE
OF FIRST PEOPLES BUFFALO JUMP

As you stand on the cliff rim at First Peoples Buffalo Jump State Park, imagine the fear and exhilaration as the ground shakes and hundreds of bison stampede past, headed toward the looming abyss.

For thousands of years, Native Americans used this buffalo jump outside of Ulm, thought to be the largest in North America, as an inventive way of hunting bison by driving them over the cliff to their ultimate demise. Tour the visitor center to learn about the importance of buffalo to tribes' way of life.

Head outside to follow the three-mile loop as it gains elevation to the base of the sandstone cliff where stairs bring you to the top. Peer down from the 50-foot cliff to look for signs of compacted bison remains below. If the walk is difficult, a short drive brings you to the top, affording 360-degree views of the surrounding plains.

342 Ulm Vaughn Rd., Ulm, 406-866-2217
fwp.mt.gov/first-peoples-buffalo-jump

OTHER BUFFALO JUMPS TO VISIT IN MONTANA

Madison Buffalo Jump State Park
6990 Buffalo Jump Rd., Three Forks, 406-285-3610
fwp.mt.gov/stateparks/madison-buffalo-jump

Wahkpa Chu'gn
1745 US Hwy. 2, Havre, 406-265-4000
buffalojumphavre.com

Historic Downtown Livingston

SHOPPING AND FASHION

STIR UP YOUR INNER CHEF
AT ZEST

Whether you fancy yourself a budding Julia Child or Jacques Pépin, or simply enjoy making the occasional home-cooked meal, you'll find every kitchen implement you'll ever need at Zest in downtown Billings.

Shop for high-end cookware and bakeware featuring brands such as Le Creuset and Emile Henry. Pick up that espresso machine you've had your eye on. Grab some essential and affordable tools to simplify your time in the kitchen, like a new set of measuring cups or a garlic press.

Zest also carries a huge variety of knife sets and cutting boards, aprons and dish towels, cleaning products, and grilling tools. Let the specialty food section inspire your next dish with unique spices and sauces from around the world. Looking to brush up on your cooking competence or learn a new recipe? Zest also offers regular classes like Sushi 101 and Introduction to Knife Skills.

110 N 29th St., Billings, 406-534-8427
zestbillings.com

SHOP 'TIL YOU DROP
AT ROCKIN RUDY'S

Rockin Rudy's is a Missoula institution. They sell a little that you need and everything you want. After over 40 years of business, Rockin Rudy's has grown into one of the largest independent retailers in the country, yet has managed to retain the cool, hip vibe Missoula is known for.

But you don't have to be cool or hip to relish a shopping trip. The inventory is varied and enormous, filling 25,000 square feet. At its core, Rockin Rudy's is a music store offering a staggering selection of CDs and records to satisfy every musical taste.

You can also shop for giggle-inducing birthday cards, candy, unique toys for kids and kids-at-heart, candles, live plants, indulgent bath products, incense, make-your-own-hot-sauce kits, apparel, ukuleles, puzzles, art projects, books, and a huge selection of unique and locally made jewelry.

237 Blaine St., Missoula, 406-542-0077
rockinrudys.com

89

PERUSE
THE POLEBRIDGE MERCANTILE

The Polebridge Mercantile sits on the northwest edge of Glacier National Park in the rugged, remote, and beautiful North Fork section of the park, just 20 miles from the Canadian border.

You can get there by either driving from the Apgar complex inside the park, or from outside the park starting in Columbia Falls. Either way, it takes some effort along dusty dirt roads, but that first bite into one of their famous huckleberry bear claws makes it all worthwhile.

The Merc is known for its baked goods, and the line in the summertime often leads out the door. Aside from the bear claws, you'll find chewy cookies, savory breads, and sandwiches perfect for sustenance on the trail. But the Merc is so much more than just a bakery. It's a general store, a community center, and the perfect place to rest with a cool drink after a long hike.

265 Polebridge Loop, Polebridge, 406-888-5105
polebridgemerc.com

READ ALL ABOUT IT
AT COUNTRY BOOKSHELF

Book lovers, rejoice as you step into Country Bookshelf, a two-story independent bookstore in the heart of Bozeman's historic downtown. This women-led literary treasure trove has been in operation since 1957 offering books on a wide range of subjects from science, cookbooks, health and wellness, travel, philosophy, fiction, and poetry.

If you're looking for a book written by a Montana author, or a book on the state's history or flora and fauna, you'll likely find it here among the shelves. If you're looking for recommendations, the staff are eager to help you find the perfect book. Still can't decide? Grab a stack and head up to the cozy nook on the top floor to peruse some options.

More than just books, Country Bookshelf also sells journals, coffee mugs, puzzles, and a number of fun gift items.

28 W Main St., Bozeman, 406-587-0166
countrybookshelf.com

DECORATE YOUR NEST
AT BIRDS & BEASLEYS

Looking to make your outdoor space a paradise for your feathered neighbors? Birds & Beasleys has you covered. This bird lovers' boutique located along the outdoor pedestrian mall at Helena's Last Chance Gulch is just the place to find all the items you need to attract wild birds to your yard. Stock up on decorative birdbaths, hummingbird feeders, feeders that hold birdseed and deter squirrels, feeders that could easily be mistaken for works of art, and plenty of birdseed to fill those feeders.

The staff is happy to answer all your questions about the backyard birds you can hope to see in Montana, and help you to attract them while keeping the birds' well-being at the forefront. While you're there, pick out items to fill your own nest with their wide selection of whimsical paintings, avian jewelry, and unique pottery, many of which were made by Montana artists.

2 S Last Chance Gulch, Helena, 406-449-0904
birdsandbeasleys.com

Birds & Beasleys

TIP YOUR HAT
TO WESTERN OUTDOOR

You can tell Western Outdoor in Kalispell is a purveyor of quality western wear when the warming smell of leather hits your nose and country music fills your ears the moment you walk in the door.

More than 1,500 hats, from straw hats to Stetsons, hang overhead in this cavernous store housed in a historic 1896 building. Browse rows of shelves stocked with more than 2,500 boots of every style, make, and color.

Shop for blue jeans durable enough for a day in the saddle and fashionable enough for a night at the rodeo. Western Outdoor carries a range of well-known brands like Tony Lama, Filson, and Minnetonka.

Friendly employees are ready to help your entire family find just what they need to work and play in the West, from oilskin duster jackets to belts and buckles, purses and blankets, clothing and shoes, games, and gifts.

48 Main St., Kalispell, 406-756-5818
westernod.com

93

FIND BARGAINS
AT PATAGONIA OUTLET

On the hunt for durable quality clothing that withstands your active outdoor lifestyle and makes you look good at a reduced price? Look no further than the Patagonia Outlet in Dillon.

For 25 years, savvy shoppers have been coming here to find screaming deals on some of the best-made outerwear on the market manufactured by a company that shares their commitment to protecting the outdoors.

Before you go, know that the outlet can offer these bargains by selling past-season clothing. This means you'll be shopping for shorts and T-shirts in the dead of winter and trying on coats when it's 90 degrees outside.

With a little planning, you'll find clothing for your outdoor adventures for half the original price, from fleece jackets to running pants to board shorts. As a bonus, they also repair Patagonia pieces you may have loved just a little too much.

16 S Idaho St., Dillon, 406-683-2580
patagonia.com/stores/mt/dillon/34-north-idaho-street/store_dillon.html

UNEARTH TREASURES
IN KEHOE'S AGATE SHOP

Make the effort to seek out this gem tucked away on a dead-end street in a residential neighborhood of Bigfork. Started in 1932 by Jack Kehoe, this jewelry and rock shop continues to be family run and features three rooms packed with fine gems, museum-worthy fossils, Montana sapphires, and minerals sourced from around the world.

Looking to impress that special someone? Try a necklace dripping with turquoise or fiery gems cradled in unique 14-karat gold settings. Wow guests to your home with a lilac amethyst geode the size of a small child.

You won't have to hunt to find fossilized cephalopods, ancient turtle shells discovered in Montana's Judith Basin, and enormous prehistoric shark teeth that put movie monsters to shame. Speaking of monsters, don't be frightened when you come upon the cave bear skeleton poised to pounce. It's just one of the many wonders you'll see at Kehoe's.

1020 Holt Dr., Bigfork, 406-837-4467
facebook.com/kehoesagateshop

PAMPER YOURSELF
AT SAGE & CEDAR

Give your skin the love and care it deserves with the natural and healthy products made by Sage & Cedar. At their two stores in Whitefish and Kalispell, you'll find a variety of lotions, bubble baths, soaps, face and hair-care products, and fragrances to suit your needs from both Sage & Cedar's signature line and other well-known brands.

Combat the dry air with almond body oil and lemongrass and sage lotion. Forget the stress of the day with a sprinkle of Let It Go bath salts followed by a dollop of peppermint and tea tree foot lotion.

A signature part of their business, Sage & Cedar offers more than 100 fragrances and essential oil blends like orange spice, Fraser fir, and sandalwood that can be added to a range of their products to create a personalized and luxurious treat made just for you.

214 Central Ave., Whitefish, 406-862-9411
227 S Main St., Kalispell, 406-890-2299
sageandcedar.com

BUY LOCAL
AT GREAT GRAY GIFTS

A visit to Great Gray Gifts is sure to put a smile on your face. Nestled beside the Ninepipes Lodge six miles south of Ronan, the shop's name and owl logo give a nod to the amazing birding opportunities right across the street at Ninepipe National Wildlife Refuge.

The retail side of Great Gray sells a range of gifts the entire family will love, many of which come from local artisans and food producers. Pick from toys and games that are both fun and educational, candles in the shape of cowboy boots, silky lotion made from goat milk, jars of honey, bags of tea, and T-shirts and sweatshirts with decorative designs celebrating the Montana way of life.

Shopping builds up an appetite and Great Gray has you covered with a selection of pastries, sandwiches, and ice cream. Be sure to grab an espresso before hitting the road.

69286 US Hwy. 93, Charlo, 406-644-2110
facebook.com/greatgraygifts

Great Gray Gifts

97

SUPPORT THE ARTISTS
OF HANDMADE MONTANA

HandMADE Montana is an organization that gives support to artisans and makers from across the state, and provides them with numerous opportunities to sell their wares. Throughout the year, HandMADE Montana puts on their wildly popular spring, summer, and holiday MADE fairs bringing hundreds of artists and makers to event centers in Helena, Bozeman, and Missoula. Wander among the booths to shop for imaginative wall art, durable yet beautiful leather goods, hand-forged knives, and exquisite pieces of jewelry, to name just a few. Half the fun is meeting the passionate artists and chatting with them about their craft. But don't fret if you can't wait for a fair. Make a visit to HandMADE Montana's brick-and-mortar store in downtown Polson, which features the work of more than 60 artists. Shop for soft woven scarves, hand-carved wooden toys, paint-by-number and embroidery kits, and stained-glass ornaments.

handmademontana.com

Retail Store
212 Main St., Polson, 406-201-9229
handmademontana.com/pages/retail-shop

98

TREAT YOUR FEET
AT HIDE & SOLE

Montanans spend quite a bit of time on our feet, whether it be hiking the trail, working in the yard, or simply seeing and being seen downtown.

No matter what your feet are doing for you today, Hide & Sole has got your back, and your feet. Hide & Sole has been a part of downtown Missoula since Scott Sproull added shoes to his custom leather goods store in 1979.

The Sole side provides a selection of a wide range of shoe styles with brands such as Haflinger, Born, Dansko, and the one that has been there since 1979, Birkenstock. The Hide side features quality leather goods used by local crafters in the making of belts, wallets, and purses.

Live in your Chacos during the summer, be prepared for the sudden rainstorm with a pair of Bogs, and stay upright crossing snowy streets in your Sorel boots.

236 N Higgins Ave., Missoula, 406-543-1128
hideandsole.com

99

SPARK CREATIVITY
AT PAPER AND GRACE

Discover the lost art of letter writing, release your inner artist, and add a flourish to any workspace at Paper and Grace, located among the boutique shops of Bozeman's historic Cannery District.

Skip the emails and put pen to paper using fine Monteverde fountain pens and colorful Crane stationery to correspond with loved ones. Prepare for a day of sketching around beautiful Bozeman with colored pencil sets, markers, and nature journals.

Pick up how-to books on calligraphy and the art of making paper flowers. Be the envy of all your coworkers and stock your desk with paper clips in the shape of forest creatures, sleek gold scissors, and vintage tins filled with French chocolates. Or simply make organization fun by scheduling your day in colorful planners and keeping track of your many writing instruments in a walrus-head pencil pot.

117 E Oak St., Ste. 1B, Bozeman, 406-577-2390
paperandgrace.com

SPEND TIME
IN DOWNTOWN LIVINGSTON

Immerse yourself in history and shop for unique gifts, home goods, outdoor gear, and fashionable clothing and accessories all at the same time in Livingston's picturesque downtown.

Livingston's profitable history hearkens back to when Polish tailor Henry Frank erected a series of ornate commercial buildings along Main Street in 1891. Remarkably, a few of the businesses that opened their doors around that time are still in operation today—like Sax & Fryer Co., purveyor of stationery, books, and art supplies, that celebrated its 140th anniversary in 2023.

Make a stop at Dan Bailey's Outdoor Company, which has been reeling in celebrities and locals to its world-renowned fly-fishing shop since 1938. Outfit your home with unique Montana decor at Wolf's Mercantile, and drop in to the Gourmet Cellar for recommendations on the perfect wine-and-cheese pairing for a picnic at nearby Sacajawea Park.

visitlivingstonmt.com/things-to-do/shopping

Flathead Lake Cherries

ACTIVITIES BY SEASON

SPRING

Brush across Western Art Week, 57

View the Art of Charlie Russell, 127

Drive the Seeley–Swan, 110

Eat Dessert First at Iron Horse Cafe & Pie Shop, 24

Migrate to Freezeout Lake, 76

Experience Native Culture at Kyiyo Pow Wow, 128

SUMMER

Pig Out at the Trout Creek Huckleberry Festival, 6

Relish the Cherries of Flathead Lake, 19

Gaze Up at the Trail to the Stars, 50

Brighten Your Day at Tizer Botanic Gardens, 46

Summer on the Slopes in Whitefish, 106

FALL

Roam with Buffalo at the Bison Range, 68

Sit a Spell at Greycliff Mill, 10

Explore the Badlands at Makoshika State Park, 66

Ramble among the Giants of Ross Creek, 104

Serve Time at Old Montana Prison, 132

Buy Local at Great Gray Gifts, 156

WINTER

Soak Up the Views at Quinn's Hot Springs, 67

Spin on the Great Northern Carousel, 36

Sip Flavors of the World at Lake Missoula Tea Company, 11

Spend Time in Downtown Livingston, 161

Celebrate the Season in Red Lodge, 51

Admire the Art of the Forest at Sculpture in the Wild, 120

Lunch at Benny's Bistro, 14

Traverse the Great Falls with the Corps of Discovery, 138

Ross Creek Cedars

Bowdoin National Wildlife Refuge

SUGGESTED ITINERARIES

DATE NIGHT

Come Home to Mission Bistro, 26

Enjoy the Bounty of Big Mountain Ciderworks, 22

Laugh until Your Sides Split at Brewery Follies, 35

Sing Along at Bigfork Summer Playhouse, 48

Rest Up at Sacajawea Hotel, 115

Believe in Mermaids at the Sip 'n Dip Lounge, 40

CREATURE COMFORTS

Greet the Animals of Yellowstone, 58

Meet the Furry Residents of Red Lodge, 56

Flock to Bowdoin National Wildlife Refuge, 78

Decorate Your Nest at Birds & Beasleys, 150

Listen to Wolves at Howlers Inn, 41

Walk on the Wild Side at ZooMontana, 42

GET ON THE WATER

Ferry across the Missouri River, 44

Voyage through Gates of the Mountains, 109

Raft through the Alberton Gorge, 101

Cruise to Wild Horse Island, 100

Swing across the Kootenai River, 102

Paddle the Clearwater Canoe Trail, 99

Relax at Sleeping Buffalo Hot Springs, 72

OFF-SEASON ADVENTURES

Feast on a Mountain at the Montana Dinner Yurt, 3

Play in the Snow at Glacier National Park, 74

Ski across Whitefish Lake Golf Course, 71

Race to Whitefish for Skijoring, 52

Shine a Light on Lewis and Clark Caverns, 107

COLLEGE TOWNS TOUR

Visit Museum of the Rockies, 130

Get Technical at American Computer & Robotics Museum, 54

Float Your Cares down the Madison River, 75

Spark Creativity at Paper and Grace, 160

Read All about It at Country Bookshelf, 149

Forage at Missoula's Farmers Markets, 27

Shop 'til You Drop at Rockin Rudy's, 147

Belly Up to Bavaria at Bayern Brewery, 4

Treat Your Feet at Hide & Sole, 159

Give a Salute to Fort Missoula, 140

Fort Benton

INDEX

American Computer & Robotics Museum, 54
Backroad Cider, 23
Bair Family Museum, 81, 142
Bannack State Park, 91, 136
Bayern Brewery, 4
Bear Paw Battlefield, 117
Benny's Bistro, 14–15
Benton Lake National Wildlife Refuge, 79
Big Arm Boat Rentals and Rides, 100
Big Hole National Battlefield, 117
Big Mountain Ciderworks, xvi, 22
Big Sky Candy, 9
Big Sky Resort, 3, 106
Bigfork Summer Playhouse, 48
Birds & Beasleys, 150–151
Bison Range, vi, 68
Bitterroot Celtic Games & Gathering, 32, 34
Bitterroot Valley Hiking Trails, 70
Blackfoot River Brewing Company, 5
Blend, 13
Blodgett Canyon Cellars, 13
Boulder Hot Springs, 73
Bowdoin National Wildlife Refuge, 78, 166
Bowman Orchards, 19
Brewery Follies, 35
Broadwater Hot Springs, 73
Busted Knuckle Brewery, 5
C. M. Russell Museum, 84, 127
Cabinet Mountain Brewing Co., 5
Candy Masterpiece Confectionery, 9
Candy Town USA, 8
Carousel for Missoula, 37
Carousel Rest Area of Shelby, 37
Charlie Russell Chew Choo, 2
Chico Hot Springs Resort & Day Spa, 73
Clark Fork River Market, 27
Clearwater Canoe Trail, 99
Country Bookshelf, 149

Cross Country Brewing, 5
Cutler Bros. Productions, 49
Daly Mansion, 34, 92, 135
Elkhorn State Park, 137
Eugene's Pizza, 30–31
Extreme History Project, The, 125
Fairmont Hot Springs Resort, 73
First Peoples Buffalo Jump, 80, 143
Flathead Lake Cheese, 7
Flathead Lake Cherries, 19, 162
Fort Benton, 87, 139, 170
Fort Benton Museum and Heritage Complex, 139
Fort Missoula Historical Museum, 140
Fort Peck Summer Theatre, 49
Freezeout Lake Wildlife Management Area, 76
Front Street Market, 21
Gallatin River Guides, 98
Garden of One Thousand Buddhas, 134
Garnet Ghost Town, 137
Gates of the Mountains Boat Tour, 89, 109
Glacier Distilling Company, 29
Glacier National Park, 74, 148
Grand Union Hotel, 139
Granite Ghost Town State Park, 137
Grant-Kohrs Ranch National Historic Site, 122
Great Gray Gifts, 156–157
Great Northern Carousel, 36
Greycliff Mill, xiv, 10
Grizzly & Wolf Discovery Center, 58
HandMADE Montana, 158
Hardtimes Bluegrass Festival, 61
Havre Beneath the Streets, 114
Headframe Spirits, 29
Helena History Tours, 125
Hidden Legend Winery, 13, 28
Hide & Sole, 159
Homestead Inn Bar & Grill, 16
Howlers Inn Bed & Breakfast and Wolf Sanctuary, 41
Iron Horse Cafe & Pie Shop, 24–25
Joe's Pasty Shop, 17
Kehoe's Agate Shop, 154
Kettlehouse Amphitheater, 38
Kootenai Falls Swinging Bridge, 102–103
Kyiyo Pow Wow, 128
Lake Missoula Tea Company, 11

Last Chance Pub & Cider Mill, 23
Last Chance Tour Train, 62
Lee Metcalf National Wildlife Refuge, 79
Lewis & Clark Trail Adventures, 101
Lewis and Clark Caverns State Park, 107
Lewis and Clark Interpretive Center, 88, 138
Little Bighorn Battlefield National Monument, 116
Livingston, Downtown, 144, 161
Lockhorn Cider House, 23
Lolo Creek Distillery, 29
Lolo Hot Springs, 73
Lone Pine State Park, 79
Madison Buffalo Jump State Park, 143
Madison River Tubing, 75
Magic City Blues Festival, 61
Makoshika State Park, 66
MAP Brewing Company, 5
Marysville Ghost Town, 137
Medicine Lake National Wildlife Refuge, 79
Mission Bistro, 26
Missoula Community Theatre, 49
Missoula's Farmers Markets, 27
Missouri Headwaters State Park, 79
Missouri River Ferries, 44–45
Montana Baroque Music Festival, 61
Montana Candy Emporium, 9
Montana Coffee Traders, 18
Montana Dinner Yurt, 3
Montana Dinosaur Center, 126
Montana Dinosaur Trail, 126
Montana Folk Festival, 60
Montana Vortex and House of Mystery, 55
MontaVino Winery & Tasting Room, 13
Montgomery Distillery, 29
Museum of the Rockies, 95, 130
Nevada City, 131
Ninepipe National Wildlife Refuge, 79, 156
Norris Hot Springs, 73
Old Butte Historical Adventures, 124
Old Montana Prison & Auto Museum Complex, 132–133
Old West Antiques & Candy Store, 9

Orchard Homes Farmers Market, 27
Paper and Grace, 160
Parrot Confectionery, 9
Pasty Place, 17
Patagonia Outlet, 153
Philipsburg Brewing Co., 5
Pictograph Cave State Park, 121
Playmill, The, 49
Polebridge Mercantile, 148
Quinn's Hot Springs Resort, 67, 96
Red Ants Pants Music Festival, 61
Red Lodge Christmas Stroll, 51
Red Lodge Songwriter Festival, 61
River's Edge Trail, 108
Roadhouse Diner, 20
Rockin Rudy's, 147
Rockin' the Rivers, 61
Rocky Mountain Museum of Military History, 141
Rosebud Battlefield State Park, 117
Ross Creek Cedars Scenic Area, 104, 165
Rough Cut Hard Cider, 23
Roy Rogers Bar Grill & Casino, 16
Ruby Valley Brew, 5
Sacajawea Hotel, 97, 115
Sage & Cedar, 155
Sculpture in the Wild International Sculpture Park, 120
Seeley–Swan Scenic Drive, 83, 110
Shed Horn Cellars, 13
Shiloh Conservation Area, 79
Sip 'n Dip Lounge, 40
Sleeping Buffalo Hot Springs, 72
Smelter City Brewing, 5
Snowbowl, 106
Southeast Montana Burger Trail, 16
Spa Hot Springs Motel, 73
Spirit of Columbia Gardens Carousel, 37
Spotted Bear Spirits, 29
Stonehouse Distillery, 29
Sweet Palace, The, 9
Sweets Barn, The, 9
Tamaracks Resort, 99
Target Range Farmers Market, 27
Ten Spoon Vineyard and Winery, 13

Tizer Botanic Gardens & Arboretum, 46
Tongue River Winery, 12
Town Talk Bakery, 17
Trail to the Stars, 50
Travelers' Rest State Park, 118–119
Trout Creek Huckleberry Festival, 6
Truzzolino Tamales, 17
Unleashed: A Winery, 13
Unseen Missoula, 125
Valhalla Meadery, 13
Virginia City, 35, 131
Virginia City Players, 35, 131
Wahkpa Chu'gn, 143
Waters Edge Winery & Bistro, 13
Western Art Week, 57
Western Cider Co., 23
Western Heritage Center, 125
Western Outdoor, 152
Westslope Distillery, 28
Whistling Andy Distillery, 29
White Raven Winery, 13
Whitefish Lake Golf Course, 71
Whitefish Mountain Resort, 106
Whitefish Skijoring, 52–53
Whitefish Winter Carnival, 52–53
Wild Horse Island, 85, 100
Wildrye Distilling, 29
Wildwood Brewing, 5
Willie's Distillery, 29
World Museum of Mining, 63, 176
Yellowstone Cellars & Winery, 13
Yellowstone Hot Springs Resort, 73
Yellowstone Wildlife Sanctuary, 56
Zest, 146
ZooMontana, 42–43

World Museum of Mining